Contents

Acknowledgements

First and foremost, this book would not be possible without the help and strength of God Almighty. Secondly, this book is also a concerted effort to bring together research, practice and information that will require further analysis and research and is only the tip of the iceberg in this rapidly developing area. I would like to pass on thanks to my family - to whom this book is largely dedicated - to my wife and to my beautiful daughters and precious son for their patience whilst I was researching and working on this publication. I would like to give special thanks to my father and mother for all the years of their support and also my brothers and sisters for their encouraging words and to all my relatives and friends

A special thank you to Andrew Nathaniel Smith for his encouraging words which were a 'divine inspiration' at times when it felt like a dead end and I required some visions to progress. Thank you to Aphton Antiona Coley for restoring my confidence during turbulent times, and for the many conversations which, unbeknown to her, gave me the motivation to continue. Thanks to Mr Mohammed Rajput for many discussions on topics such as Islam, Quran and traditions. Also to my many colleagues for the various discussions and insight on topics such as terrorism, Islam, Christianity, religion, social work, politics, history and criminology. Especially, to those that encouraged this publication and that saw a need for something to be published in this particular area. To those from the Apostolic Church for help with the difficult theological aspects that required interpretation and clarification. And to the many discussions with the many academics and professionals that have helped me shape and direct this publication. I hope all those professionals, practitioners, academics, researchers and organisations working with children and young people will get to understand this subject, its issues and concerns, better and to take the points discussed in this material seriously. Finally, the errors that remain, which I pray are minor, are purely mine alone.

Safeguarding from extremism

a new approach post 7/7

JASWANT SINGH BOORA

Published by Paragon Publishing

ISBN 978-1-78222-396-2

Book design, layout and production management by Into Print
www.intoprint.net
+44 (0)1604 832149

Printed and bound in UK and USA by Lightning Source

Introduction

*'This country will be absolutely resolute in its stand against violent extremism
and terror and that confronting extremism is a job for us all'.*

David Cameron, 2013.

'When I grow up I want to be a terrorist' says a young child whilst drawing a picture in a school. These frightening words are the self-expressions of a 10 year old child from the UK. Indeed, these expressions show that children and young people in general are becoming more familiar with terms and words that are repeatedly shaped and fostered in a world in which the news is dominated by terrorism and global conflict. What is even more alarming, however, is the reality that extremist ideology and propensity to adopt terrorist thinking have become more blended within the fabric of mainstream society and, increasingly, people holding such views are of British origin. The shocking footage of the seemingly random killing of a solider near Woolwich Barracks by Islamist extremists in 2013, took matters to new heights. The TV coverage of the brutal murder of Drummer Lee Rigby on the streets of Britain astonished a whole nation, sending further reverberations all over the world. The message was clear and for those living in the UK the indelible question that arose, who next? His death certainly assured many, that in no uncertain terms, that a different form of religious violence had gripped the UK. The Prime Minister David Cameron would respond in a statement outside Number 10 *this country will be absolutely resolute in its stand against violent extremism and terror* and *that confronting extremism is a job for us all'*[1].

The growing problem of extremism has continued to dominate international news ever since the terrorist attacks on September 11th 2001. Needless to say, this has led to numerous inquisitions. The brutal nature of violent extremism and terrorism required a unified response, especially within the wider context of safeguarding vulnerable individuals within the UK. On the point of safeguarding, one report had also stated that in one case, a father convicted of terrorism, was heard on tape recording during an interview indoctrinating his five year old son with terrorist material. More pointedly, in 2014, in light of the so-termed 'Trojan Horse Plot' serious concerns arose about the threat of Islamic extremists taking over 25 academies in

---

1   David Cameron, speech 10 Downing Street, 13th June 2013 https://www.gov.uk/government/speeches/statement-on-woolwich-incident

Birmingham, West Midlands. The presence of a counter-terrorism officer increased the demand to explore these and other safeguarding concerns at the school. Ofsted Investigations would follow. The metropolitan anti-terror unit, headed by its chief Peter Clarke, acquired the responsibility for analysing the evidence in relation to these concerns. Of course, questions began to emerge, especially from political figures, the wider community and professionals with commitments to safeguarding children and young people. Some of these questions were centered on this issue and other terrorist attacks that have materialised in the UK, for example; what effects did the actions of extremists have on British children and young people watching? How were these actions of violent extremists interpreted by children and young people, positive or negative? And more importantly for those professionals with responsibility for protecting children and young people, what were the wider dangers espoused to the welfare of this vulnerable groups in terms of the unforeseen risks and threats and from the increasing and current problems surrounding the recruitment and the radicalisation of children and young people? In this sense, what seems to be lacking, since the terrorist attacks in 2005, is a thorough and informed examination that offers a context to why and how this is happening, especially within a country that has gained an international reputation for developing and applying strong security measures and tight monitoring procedures, especially in terms of safeguarding children and young people, which shall be explored in chapter one.

This timely book seeks to address, and more specifically, to contextualise the period covering the terrorist attacks in 2005 to the present day by focusing on the current risk and threats posed to children and young people. Here it is conceived that this also relates to the safeguarding of vulnerable children and young people from extremism. It also seeks to entertain and open up the various discussions, expositions and views surrounding the profound nature of safeguarding with an intention to invite and arouse further discussions on aspects pertaining to the 'maltreatment' and 'abuse' of children and young people as an 'uncharted territory' within the landscape of extremism. Its originality, due to the limited research and literature, not on safeguarding per se, but on safeguarding from extremism, in academia and elsewhere, has presented many challenges for professionals, particularly for social workers and other professionals protecting vulnerable children and young people. For many, it is difficult to grasp this rapidly emerging phenomenon within a concise, coherent and methodical context. Considerable information and literature has, over time, been eagerly acquired and transmitted from disciplines such as: politics, law, history, criminology, youth work, social psychology, theology and religion in desperate attempts to provide understanding, defining and addressing the problems of extremism, violent extremism and terrorism. This has also proven to be problematic and again, cause many to re-boot their efforts to continue to search for concrete answers.

In this sense, this study is also geared towards fulfilling these gaps by sharing these challenges in practice and by exploring the current and developing reviews, publications, policies and frameworks between government agendas on safeguarding and CONTEST (counter-terrorism), with a view to conflate together within this material. In some ways, safeguarding is not a new word; however, safeguarding from extremism on the other hand, requires a thorough analysis given the disturbing nature by which it has now enlarged due to the determinative motor of the exocentricity of terrorism. This book does not positively aspire to give any concrete answers or solutions in resolving this matter, nor does it imply or suggest that it holds any monopoly on this subject, but instead, seeks to invoke and provide a fresh basis and review in light of this study and to contribute to this subject. It will also attempt to encourage positive synergies between services, agencies and organisations with a view to exchanging information on this basis. For those within social work or related disciplines, I appreciate that language used may cause some turbulence, but this is inevitable, given the readers may not have come across such a vocabulary before, which will no doubt, raise further question pertaining to its relevance. On this point, I will also stress to the readers that this book will also introduce many to an entirely new use of concepts and vocabulary as they progress and where they will see its essential linkage to this subject and material. This will also enable readers to grasp the importance of why this research has been presented. As this becomes visible, this will invoke and stimulate dialogue enabling us to distinguish between what is government policy and what has been recommended. It is also the author's intention to clarify use of terms within this book. It has also come to light that other factors, on this agenda are inextricably linked and which is largely underdeveloped.

For example, a child and young person's emotional and psychological well-being were seriously affected as a result of direct exposure to extremist environments and interactions. This had diverse ramifications on children and young people development. These points are discussed throughout this material. Another disturbing, yet prolific aspect of extremism advancement was seen with the complexity surrounding the radicalisation of children and young people. This has and continues to complicate matters further. Initially, these bewildered many to how and where extremist managed to groom and recruit them. Some of these avenues may not yet have been thoroughly explored or even yet identified, though many citations have been made already to soothe our understanding. Notwithstanding this, we are also informed through research pertaining to the voluntary choices of young people to engage in extremism or terrorism activity. These developments must also be given a stage to vocalise their findings, seeming they are but a plausible one, which appear to offer some scope and valuable insight. These points have been expounded in research by advocates such as Professor Joe Cole from the University of Liverpool. Because of these and the aforementioned views, the fight against extremism and terrorism in the UK is one that is often unpredictable and that can be misleading. In expounding upon how this can be responded too, Dr Steve Hewitt offers some contribution. His emphasis is one of prevention, informing us that fundamentally, we must keep *terrorists, who will always exist, marginalised and on the edges of the community they operate*. These are points that are further expounded upon in the forthcoming coming chapters.

The moral obligations of extremists encouraged some to relocate. By doing so, they have found a 'safe haven' to live and operate within the UK. This created an open access, enabling them to find new recruits. At bare minimum this book also seeks to contribute towards providing an endocentric understanding towards the practicalities of safeguarding children and young people form these threats, even within family settings. This has tenable relevance. I must remind the readers that violent extremists and terrorists are a threat to any democratic order and it is impossible to put a precise figure on how many are hidden or lurking within our society, though many researchers and academic may attempt to provide figures or estimations, which in my view, are not accurate by reasons of the current extremism climax, especially in terms of changes and transitions due to global events of terrorism. These tend to fluctuate at a rapid rate.

It would be the terrorist attacks in London during 2005 that shifted the emphasis, providing a new impetus. The direct actions of 'four home grown' British terrorists, a new term in itself due to these suicide bombings, prompted many to re-interpret the threat posed to the British public not just simply as serious but as 'life threatening'. MI5, the British Security services would respond. The threat of home-grown terrorism was a point already highlighted early in 2005 by the then junior home office minister Hazel Bloom. She had warned us that home grown terrorism had become a bigger threat than from those abroad. And let's not forget, that years prior to the London bombings, in July 2000 a security service operation, codenamed LARGE, uncovered the first Islamist bomb factory to be detected in Britain supporting suspicions that the UK was a target. It is hardly surprising, that on the 29th August 2014, MI5 would raise the threat level to 'SEVERE' on their website, which indicates that a terrorist attack is highly likely to happen.

Since the attacks in 2005 and even prior, terrorist groups have continued to espouse themselves towards new heights of physical violence and in this sense, the track records of terrorist groups have continued to enlarge. The inhumane killing of 141 children, including teachers, by the extremist group called the Taliban, has opened past wounds and certainly inflicted new ones. The 'Pakistan School Massacre' which took place in the city of Peshwar, Pakistan during December 2014 , serves as reminder of the 'raw evil' that extremist groups are capable of inflicting, and in the tearful words of Dr Asif Sohrah after this attack he states 'Peshwar bleeds, Pakistan cries'. These particular motives were driven by revenge in retaliation to the ongoing military conflicts between the Pakistani army and the Taliban. Possessing prior knowledge that the children of those officers working for the Pakistan army attended this Northern-run school, opened up a perfect opportunity to inflict deep emotional, physical and psychological pain, which we can all empathise with will last for many years to come. As it did with 9/11, the reasons and root causes behind these attacks and other uncertainties required clarification. It has been noted that there are at least 100 definitions of terrorism that attempt to unpack these uncertainties. This further complicates our decision to agree a singular definition and leads to another burning question, which has generated a tremendous sense of expectation worldwide: why does terrorism happen?

In a famous publication by Martha Crenshaw in 1981, *The Roots of Terrorism,* Crenshaw explains how the terrorism stage is set for a particular purpose over a prolonged period of time. She refers to these prerequisites as the *'preconditions and root causes'*[2]. On the latter point, many trigger points have been held responsible for these occurrences, one example being revenge, as seen in the school massacre above. As difficult as it may be and for the purpose of this study, we will need to arrive at a general consensus on agreeing a particular definition. There are numerous contributions that are at our immediate disposal. Most, if not all definitions on terrorism have arrived at a general consensus that assert, *'terrorism is a conscious act of the people involved',* whereas, *'radicalisation is a process of socialisation which*

---

2   The Roots of Terrorism, Crenshaw, 1981.

people go through that could, ultimately but not necessarily, bring them to acts of terrorism' Given these consumptions, I will also inform the readers, that most definitions will incorporate some assumptions regarding how a person is recruited and subsequently radicalised, which are open to debate and discussion. This is further examined in chapter three. Whilst engaged on the delivering counter-terrorism work, I have often pondered on these and other extremist interactions, which have reminded me of my theological views pertaining to the manifold behaviours of mankind, which are equally as disturbing. These have their origins. It is worth keeping these points in mind, given the subject matter of this book - points that will be promulgated throughout this study. This then draws our attention to the terrorist attacks in 2005.

The government's responses to the terrorist attacks were swift. The government's counter-terrorism strategy introduced in 2003 was called CONTEST. The strategy contained the numerous expressions and responses to this product. These were presented in the form of; Peruse, Prepare, Protect and Prevent. It would be the Prevent strand that would focus its responses towards supporting frontline services and organisations primarily for prevention purposes. These were categorised into Prevent objectives. Prevent possessed very little powers of enforcement or arrest, focusing on support. The revised strategy published by the Home Office in June 2011, which is discussed in more detail in chapter four, would reinforce this notion, particularly objective two of the strategy, which stipulated that *'Supporting vulnerable individuals who are targeted and recruited to the cause of violent extremism'*[3]. This has become a critical component to counter-terrorism work. This was more simply said than done. There was another component that was critical to the fight against extremism and one that fitted well in disrupting extremist intentions. This was seen with inter-agency responses. This was an crucial component to preventing extremism, which is discussed further in chapter five. Another drastic innovation saw a police-led project called Channel, set up in 2006 by ACPO (Association of Chief Police Officers). This venture was intriguing and began to open up scope. This generated interest and transformed many organisations. In addition to the channel project, other requirements were needed to assist with this emerging dynamic. This also helped to develop, establish and sustain long-term relationships between agencies that had a vested interest in persuing best practice. For example, a document produced in 2010 entitled Prevent

---

3   HM Prevent Strategy 2011.

and Safeguarding demonstrated this relationship and supplied the knowledge that was so desperately needed to prepare and equip professionals. This was also a concerted effort to bring together a range of services that were expected to safeguard children and young people from the dangers of extremism. These proliferations were intriguing, in that they were expected to be correlative, particularly by bringing together key players such as Local Safeguarding Children Boards (LSCBs) and the Prevent agenda towards a unified approach.

It was also becoming clearer that some British nationals were playing a more significant role in these threats. These concerns prompted major reforms. As part of these reforms, terrorism laws were hurried through parliament. Of course, government intervention would prove integral to the overall responses as would the need to build trust with the wider community, especially for the purpose of engagement. For the benefit of the readers, the causes of terrorism in the UK predate 2005. British citizens have been known to engage in acts of terrorism dating as far back as 1881; this is explored further in chapter two. Prior to the July 7th terrorist attacks, the first British citizen involved in suicide bombings was a young man named Khalid Shahid. While fighting in Afghanistan in 1996 he asked members of the Taliban to hide grenades in his jacket which he could detonate when the northern alliance tried to arrest him. To add insult to injury, extremists have launched multiple campaigns in the UK in drastic attempts to recruit vulnerable individuals to engage in acts of violence and terrorism. Because of this, attempts to protect those vulnerable individuals in addition to the wider public, have complicated matters further and in the case of Drummer Lee Rigby, serve as a reminder, that violent extremists have very little compassion for their victims. In efforts to curtail and disrupt extremists, the use of revised terrorism laws was a uniformed response to terrorism in the UK; though needed, brought with it additional and unexpected problems. One of the most obvious was the 'violation of liberty' in the form of breaching 'Human Rights'. This angered many humanitarian groups, one being Liberty.

To date, the youngest person convicted of terrorism offences in the UK would be a young man from Yorkshire named Hammad Munshi. Aged just 15 years old at the time, his radicalisation would take place whilst at school. Similarities have been compared with known cases in the US. An article in the Baltimore Sun stated that a case in Howard's County (in Philadelphia) refers to a young man named Mohammed Hassan Khalid,-a man brought to America from Pakistan by his father,-who was arrested on terrorism charges. The 18 year old became one of the youngest people ever to be convicted in federal court in America of conspiracy to aid terrorists. It was later established that he started engaging in terrorism activities whilst at high school aged just 15 years old. Like the case in the US, it is here that shades of safeguarding children and young people from extremism required greater focus and responses.

The London terrorist attack in 2005 was also a cause to ventilate strong emotions. These were geared towards protecting Britain from extremism and from the 'islamification' of the wider British population. This replacement was in danger of banishing British values to the peripheries, if not out of existence. The slow progress of the British government to effectively respond to the so termed 'Islamic threat of extremism' was observed by many as the fear to respond to the exceptional dominance of Islam that was viewed as attempting to control and transform democracy. This gave conception to opposing far-right groups that sought to neutralise these foes. The most notorious being the EDL. The EDL (English Defence League), which formed in 2009, offered the British public alternatives and sought to thrust matters beyond the reach of political spheres. These social thrusts were acted out through a series of demonstrations and marches in cities all over the UK (one major march being in the city of Birmingham in 2009) and were often portrayed alongside acts of violence and criminality. In defending their position, a statement made by the EDL they have repeatedly argued that, *'due to the frustration at the lack of any significant action by the British government against extremist Muslim preachers and organisations... We have had enough of our government ignoring both the problem itself and the cries for action from the majority of those in this country'*[4] Of course, these particular settings appealed to many young people whose physical presence at these locations gave credence to safeguarding concerns. These social situations presented ideal opportunities for young people to engage in violent and problematic behaviour in the name of, and defence of, British values. Further fragmentations have also occurred since 2005.

Some of the tensions that exist between our religious and racial communities have also been a consequence of the terrorist attacks. These attacks provided the opening that gave oxygen to fuel grievances which were exacerbated by political parties and directed against certain groups. For example, terms frequently used such as 'foreigners' and 'immigrants' became predominant vocabulary amongst opposing groups such as the BNP (British National Party). Needless to say, this has added fuel to the fire. In the firmament of

---

4   UK 2009 Rundown: A year of Fire and Ice.

an enclosed setting, the preservation of 'British values' and 'White children heritage' were highly contagious arguments, reflecting the BNP and its leader Nick Griffin, political, social and ideological stance, who himself has a conviction for inciting racial hatred and has even denied the holocaust. His condescending remarks against these communities were loaded with negative connotations, some that indicated that the British government was perceived as yielding towards 'ethnic groups' and more specifically, to 'Muslim communities' and the preferences given to these through opportunities such as social housing, benefits and jobs, over their white British-born counterparts, escalated indignation in the hearts of the British people. These orientations were designed to alter British perceptions. His deliberate use of these opposing citations, paid off, influencing many to disengage and withdraw themselves from integrating on these grounds. His messages certainly acquired momentum, instantly taking root within the minds of the general population. Unrepentant, the BNP's intimidation tactics sought to discourage others. An article published by the *Daily Telegraph* in March 2014, highlighted concerns about Muslim infiltration into other recreational settings. After long talks with Thames Valley Police they had forced Legoland to close for an entire weekend, after threats were issued, when they found out that this popular destination had been booked by a radical Muslim cleric who intended to have a Muslim fun day. In response to this, a British National Party blogger said Legoland should be *'ashamed of themselves for bowing to these Muslims'.* Moreover, the blog added *'this is disgusting and should not be allowed to go ahead'*[5]. It is also necessary to point out that certain groups, ethnic or not, can also become the 'victims of public or political opinions'. These opinions in the wrong place can and if fuelled by the wrong individuals could be damaging.

In the immediate aftermath of 7/7, serious concerns arose that many, including young people, were at risk of becoming radicalised by extremists to engage in violent acts of terrorism against the UK. MI5, the British security service, also believed that in 2007, an estimated 2,000 random individuals posed a direct threat to national security and public safety. The previous MI5 chief, Jonathan Evans responsible for informing the wider security sectors, disclosed that, *'extremists were methodically and intentionally targeting young people and children in the UK, and that groups like Al-Qaeda were recruiting children as young as 15 years old to wage a deliberate campaign of terror in Britain'*[6]. Moreover, in his first memorable speech as director, Mr

---

5   Telegraph 2014.

6   MI5 Jonathan Evans 2007.

Evans warned that extremists were *'radicalising, indoctrinating and grooming young, vulnerable people to carry out acts of terrorism,'* and that urgent action was required on the part of the UK government, *'to protect its children from exploitation by violent extremists'.* The former director of the CIA (Central Intelligence Agency, USA) Michael Hayden, has previously stressed that Al-Qaeda is actively seeking youths from western countries because of their familiarity with the language, culture and appearance (such as the 7/7 bombers) and would therefore, as he states, *'not illicit any notice whatsoever, from you if they were standing next to you in the airport.* With this in mind it is hardly surprising that Al-Qaeda has referred to children in the past as the, *'new generation of Mujahidin'*, and according to statistics, estimates suggest that youths between 15-18 years old make up about 20 per cent of all suicide bombers. The current problem of ISIS (Islamic State) has intensified matters further This impact has not only been felt within the UK but elsewhere in neighbouring countries.

From March 11th, 2012 an Al-Qaeda killing spree in the cities of Toulouse and Montauban Southern France, targeted a Jewish school, killing a French soldier, a teacher and four children. This was compounded with the actions of the French government that were held responsible for many French young people embracing the pursuit of jihad in countries such as Syria. This was linked with the idea of a military defence against a French invasion of Syria, a point already stressed by the International Centre for the Study of Radicalisation based in the UK. Furthermore, France's stance of addressing violent extremism head-on reinforces the notion that the threat of 'home grown terrorism' may be very much alive. With the options available, French authorities would focus their efforts by adopting an inter-agency response to addressing extremism. This venture incorporated schools, parents and the wider local Muslim community. Similarly, Boris Rhein, the interior minister of the western state of Hesse, is alarmed by the growing numbers of German jihadists making their way to Syria to take up arms in civil war. The rise in the number of young German Muslims going to Syria in 2014 has compelled German intelligence agencies to investigate further. In one particular case, a 26 year old man called, Burak Karan, made German headlines. Karan had once been a promising soccer play from North Rhine, Germany and had played for the German under 16s and 17s. He had played with likes of Kevin-Prince Boateng as a teammate, yet he was deprived of his young inspiring talent. Eventually radicalised, Karan would head for Syria, where he would be killed. In Belgium an estimated 30-85 jihadists are fighting in the country, the youngest aged 18 years who was converted to Islam at the age of 15 years old. As far as religious teachings are concerned, it is quite obvious that some Islamist extremists have ignored their own teachings in favour of full-scale offensive jihad as the only option to resolving matters, irrespective of the environment or social conditions. By doing so, they have not only shown blatant disregard for the God given liberty to others but have gone beyond limits by reason of 'diminished responsibility' to their own self-destruction. This has dire consequences. For example, it was stressed by the prophet Muhammad, *'beware of extremism in religion, for it was extremism that destroyed those who went before you'*.

The consecutive decisions and quasi-intellect of extremists over-powered the most vulnerable and sought to render others powerless. This required a drastic response. Moreover, the catastrophic events of 7/7 compelled a majority of professionals from a range of disciplines working with children and young people to be *'fast tracked'* through a series of training distributed and distributed by the Home office and YJB (Youth Justice Board) especially during the earlier periods in 2008, 2009 and 2010. Having attended these and other independent training programmes, has at times has caused many to question some of the materials presented at the time as a scholastic effort to explain the fundamentals of religions such as Islam, though, some appreciation must be given here for its wider relevance and practical application, but for the many consumers, I suppose it has left a blank canvas. Throughout my observations, the wider implications to the safeguarding of children and young people from extremism were at times avoided and lacking. This led to dead ends. This was another challenge allotted to the Home Office and Local Safeguarding Children Boards (LSCBs) to come up with the goods. These voids led to another emerging dynamic in this counter-terrorism and safeguarding venture. This was evident with the intriguing innovation between safeguarding and Prevent's uniformity. In the aftermath of 7/7, the dispatch of the Prevent agenda has seen tremendous growth and is steering towards pole position as a preferred approach. Certainly, very few were able to contest its authority, with its powers deriving from the Home Office, which has to a certain extent demanded compliance. This also shortened proximity, allowing services to come together. Needless to say, there were also wider social work implications to these proposals.

It wouldn't be long before political figures entered the social care realms and 'rustled the feathers' of professionals regarding the issues of safeguarding

---

7   Prophet Muhammad.

children from extremism. *'Radicalisation is a form of child abuse and the authorities must have more power to intervene'* said the Mayor of London, Boris Johnson. He elaborates, *'There is built in the British system a reluctance to be judgemental about some else's culture even if that reluctance places children at risk'* and *'we are familiar by now with the threat posed by preachers of hate, the extremist clerics who can sow seeds of medicine in the minds of impressionable young people'* in the same breath *'We know the problem of radicalisation is not getting conspicuously worse - but nor is it going away. What has been less widely understood is that some young people are now being radicalised at home, by their parents or their step-parents'* It could be estimated there could be hundreds of children. *At present, there is a reluctance by the social services to intervene, ever when key and the police have clear evidence of what is going on because it's not clear that the 'safeguarding law' would support such action, The Law should obviously treat radicalisation as a form of child abuse'.* He continues to stress, *'it is estimated that there could be hundreds of children who are being taught crazy stuff',* and *'a child may be taken into care if he or she is being exposed to pornography, or is being abused - but not if the child is being habituated to this utterly bleak and nihilistic view of the world that could lead them to become murderers'.* In short, his exposition was explicit, suggesting that a firmer approach was needed in preventing children from succumbing to extremism and were reflective of another innovative venture that was in the pipeline.[8] In this sense, exceptional social care responses were required as was the need for tailored assessments that were reflective on a wide range of factors to help accomplish this task. One particular candidate already in circulation was highly favoured for this task. In its nomination, the CAF (Common Assessment Framework) provided the necessary apparatus for professionals to climb towards this goal. Given these fresh narratives, developing themes have begun to resonate within childcare sectors. These significations are expounded upon in the forthcoming chapters.

Since the terror attacks on September 11th 2001 and because of the tactics and the degree of violence already used by violent extremists and terrorist that assures us of their intentions, it has compelled the British governments to introduce a range of counter-measures, policies and especially, counter-terrorism departments to be installed. These have been seen with the following departments that have been introduced. In 2003 the 'Joint Terrorist Analysis Centre' was formed, in response to 7/7 attacks and for the purpose of community engagement RICU 'Research Information Communication Unit

---

8   Mayor of London, Boris Johnson 2014.

– based in the Home Office was set up in 2007, in 2013 given the problems of social media, extremism and recruitment the 'Extreme Task Force' was set up by David Cameron and with the most recent seen with 'Due Diligence and Counter Extremism Group' set up in 2014, with the appointment of Rosemary Pratt as its current director. The requirement for services to adjust to accommodate these new counter-terrorism measures became a critical juncture in the process as was the proposed service convergence, which is discussed in chapter five. These transitions formed the basis towards promoting better-informed outcomes. In addition to this, multiple strategic and operational meetings were conveyed to consider more effective ways to safeguard children from extremism and terrorism. This was a significant development in a number of respects and required the expert input from CTU (Counter Terrorism Unit), a task initially beyond the scope and capacity of Local Safeguarding Children Boards (LSCBs). And yet, for many working with children and young people, safeguarding is not a relatively new word within social work and other circles, but since the attacks has created further challenges to safeguard in this new context. This is discussed in detail in the opening chapter. On another note, I will stress here, having spent some time on delivering this agenda, this whole venture was initially problematic and was only the start to a prolonged, unpredictable and exhausting journey. Moreover, having listened to the advice from the many, in my view 'commentators of extremism' were at times, monotonous and had very little currency amongst those that possessed the broader expertise, skills or knowledge from a wide range of professions and disciplines. On this point, the imposition of a narrow uniformity requires constant elaboration within this new context, especially for those in the social work and related disciplines This also involves even more now post 7/7, the urgency to employ those with the relevant skills and knowledge and expertise to deliver credible and effective interventions, not just within a religious or theological context. These points will become clearer throughout this material.

With that said, we will open our journey in chapter one by giving an historical overview of safeguarding within the UK and to set a context leading up to July 7th bombings. This will be the foundation where the safeguarding agendas will have their formal transition into counter-terrorism work. It is here that we shall briefly explore other interesting notions such as defining extremism, introduction of terrorism legislation, the adverse effects this will have on the child development and exploring the wider issues of abuse and maltreatment of children because of the dangers of being exposed to violent extremism. In chapter two I shall give a brief account of the historical context of terrorism in the UK this will open further discussion within this historical context. A key one being theology. This chapter will discuss the security concerns, in terms of past and current threats to the UK. The international scope that is discussed will help us to understand if such problems are globally shared or exclusive to the UK and to what extent the notion of 'home grown terrorism' is thriving and to explore to what extent young people are playing a role in these home grown threats. Chapter three shall attempt to offer some definitions of terrorism and radicalisation, its process and some of the research and theories that underpin this, especially in terms of recruitment, that are specific to children and young people, giving case studies where necessary. These will include psycho-social and criminological theories and introduce health and medical factors, opening room for further discussions, debate and research. I will also explore if radicalisation has some historical significance. Chapter four will inform us of the current Prevent agenda, its objectives, scope, reviews and problems. This will also form the basis to explore the relationship that currently exists, and has gradually developed between safeguarding and Prevent. This will be of particular interest to social workers, teachers and other like-minded professionals and inform us of things to come. The final chapter will explore the importance of inter-agency working as a means to combat extremism and terrorism sustained through collaborative and holistic responses. This will cover aspects such as obligations to safeguard, statutory legislation, Prevent's role, effective systems, challenges and consideration for other sectors, giving international perspectives on similar approaches where necessary. This will also introduce the expertise contributed by Prevent professionals within existing services; although some problems have also been identified with this since 2005, which will be highlighted. This will be summarised with my conclusions, which will help to plan for the future.

To help familiarise readers, I will briefly share my personal experiences. I must stress here, that my professional practice, experience and qualifications have assisted with this publication. My skills and knowledge have been largely acquired whilst working with children and young people over many years within a wide range of disciplines and roles. Some of these have included the following roles: youth offending officer, senior youth worker, preventing violent extremism officer and management. In addition, I have also been a visiting lecturer at Birmingham City University (security and criminal justice) and am also a professionally qualified trainer, with experience of training a range of professionals. I have also participated in a range of training sessions on extremism and terrorism, including those delivered by the Youth Justice Board and Office of Security and Counter-Terrorism. Others have been in collaboration with organisations such as the DCSF (Department of Children, Schools and Families) now DfE (Department of Education) and a master class and residential delivered by the Recora Institute. I have also attended OSCT consultations on the Prevent agenda in 2010 and attended terrorism legislation consultation during the same year. This has enabled me to deliver focused work on a one to one and group basis with children and young people, especially within the youth justice system and education sectors. I have also been instrumental in developing, organising and hosting conferences for all nations consultancy on issues such as racism, extremism and terrorism. These have included 'Preventing Violent Extremism - a Practitioner's Approach in 2011' at the Police training centre, Tally Ho, Birmingham and Addressing the Many Forms of Violent Extremism in 2012. In collaboration with other institutions during 2013 I have organised events such as 'Prevent, policy and legislation' 2013 with the University of Buckinghamshire and the 'Race and hate crime' in Birmingham during 2013. These events have incorporated a wide range of guest speakers including Lord Carlyle (previous independent reviewer and government advisor on terrorism legislation 2001-2011). I have spoken on the subject of extremism and terrorism on Sky Asian network channel Sangat TV.

1: From Safeguarding to Extremism

'The Welfare of the Child is paramount'

Section 1 Children Act 1989.

Before I proceed to explore the complexities of safeguarding children and young people from extremism post 7/7 it is at this earliest starting point that this subject will require some input from the world of safeguarding. This is necessary and will help to set out some key distinctions. The purpose of this will, essentially, enable readers to comprehend some of the following, which shall set the tenor of the discussion for the forthcoming chapters. Firstly, appreciate the reasons why we need to safeguard children and young people, given the current concerns; this will also help to set a context. Secondly, to explore the diversified effect of the July 7th 2005 London terrorist attacks that has given credence to the various counter-terrorism reviews, publications, reforms and formations. Thirdly, how services have attempted to incorporate the numerous imperatives of government recommendation to tackle violent extremism and terrorism. Some of these advancements have been apparent through partnership and inter-agency working, Home Office consulta-tions and counter-terrorism training that prior to the terrorist attacks were somewhat scarce. This was another interesting venture in itself. It is envis-aged that this research will drive forward the potential to encourage readers towards 'new heights of thinking and engagement'; this will particularly influ-ence those engaged with children and young people, for example the many social work and care professionals, organisations, managers. This will also influence many towards actively engaging on this counter-terrorism agenda with a view to safeguard the next generation of children and young people from extremism.

SAFEGUARDING - A DEVELOPING AGENDA

The sheer volume of child abuse concerns and scandals, over the years, has informed us that the need to safeguard children has become even more paramount. This and other modalities have their origins. Early examples of its determinative function can be dated as far back as the early 16th century, if not further. During this period, key responsibility for accommodating and promoting the welfare of children (predominately orphans at the time) stemmed from ecclesiastical institutions such as the Church. Diachronically, the emerging and unexpected problems that would present themselves during this early period in reference to the broader safeguarding challenges would prove too complex for these institutions to manage given their limited scope. This required drastic intervention and action, in terms of protection, and because of the complex nature in these dynamics it was a task that was better performed and suited for others. This would come in the form of legislation and was imperative to secure a child well-being. It would not be over-enthusiastic to suggest that the 'prayers of the church' would eventually be answered. In this sense, a confluence of promising measures arose. In 1889 the 'prevention of cruelty to and protection of children act' and 'children's charter' would be passed by parliament. Police could now arrest anyone mistreating a child and enter homes to prevent children from danger. During these interactions, the urgency to take action against these injustices continued to be given priority. These judicial reforms were dramatic as well as explosive and in recognition of this, prompted a series of childcare legislation that rapidly evolved. It would also be in 1889 that we would see the formation of the NSPCC (National Society for the Prevention of Cruelty to Children) and the early form of the Children Act 1908 would come onto the scene. Prior to these promising measures, it was the 'poor law' introduced in 1700 that was the primary legislation that was responsible and tasked with protecting the welfare of children. This legislation would remain active until it was formally ended with the Children act 1948.

The Infant Life (preservation) Act 1929'[9] was instrumental in recognising early forms of harm, even prior to birth. In reference to the cruelty against children and young people, the acquisition of one most notable legislation still widely used today 'the children and young person act 1933' recognised the need to protect children from neglect as showcased in section one of the act that prevented '*causing ill-treatment or neglect*'[10]. During the mid-40s the death of a young child, Denis O'Neil, at the hands of foster carers led to the Monckton inquiry in 1945 and to the reports of Curtis and Clyde committees. These reports were critical, especially in reference to the handling of this case and identified key failures that were contributory and that could of prevented his death, these included '*public authority care for children and weakness in administration and supervision*'[11]. The outcome of this report culminated in the Children Act 1948. The Act codified childcare functions within the Home Office by ensuring that issues addressing

---

9   The Life Preservation Act 1929.

10   The Children and Young Persons Act 1939.

11   The National Archives 1915-1984 (Cabinet Papers).

child welfare were 'well on the radar'. This also demanded the creation of separate departments in local authorities to respond to children at risk. This accelerated the social work profession. As a result of this advancement, in 1971 social services department were installed. This opened a new dispensation that widened up the scope and one that sought to regulate matters through these new departments. However, in spite of promising venture, this could not prevent further failures.

In 1973, the death of Maria Colwell gained national media coverage, compelling numerous inquiries and investigations into her death. The *Report of the Committee of Inquiry into the Care and Supervision Provided in Relation to Maria Colwell* chaired by Thomas Gilbert Field Fisher, a Recorder of the Crown Court, identified three main contributory factors involved in these failures: the lack of communication between the agencies who were aware of her vulnerable situation; inadequate training for social workers assigned to at-risk children; and changes in the make-up of society. Summing up, he emphasised, *'It is not enough for the State as representing society to assume responsibility for those such as Maria'*. This would lead to significant changes the following year that would dictate how child protection was practiced. These rebukes were taken seriously. This was promising. This gave credence to introduce in 1970' what many professionals have become acquainted with today and which then, became known as 'case conferences. This also saw the 'at risk' register come into force.

Indeed, it is precisely because of these disturbing patterns that the creation of distinct teams were mobilised with a primary focus to safeguard and protect vulnerable children. These governmental thrusts gave credence for the local authorities to introduce ACPCs (Area Child Protection Committees) though long overdue, were welcomed. Other cardinal signs emerged. The need to remove or relocate a child to a secure location would also be given similar treatment. One could suggest that all danger has passed; this could not be further than the truth. A few years later, in 1985, the death of a young girl, Jessica Beckford, became the final straw, suggesting that 'enough was enough' - this drove forward change. Ongoing reviews and reports (one being the Cleveland report in 1988 pertaining to issues of 'child sexual abuse') during these turbulent times, demonstrated governments intentions to invoke radical overhauls in desperate attempts to counter these failures and to ensure that child safety was polarised. This culminated with the introduction of the 'Children Act 1989' a notorious landmark in the fight to safeguard and protect vulnerable children and young people. This enabled and encouraged interactions from a wide range of services and disciplines to access its content. This legislation certainly filled a gap. It would eventually become the quintessential of all child care legislation. Many professionals reciprocated as a result. The volume of legislation (ten bills in total) was a testament of the government's promise to deliver. The Children Act 1989 was also responsible for replacing the 'at risk' register introduced in 1974 with the 'child protection register'.

The 1989 Act provided the UK with a revolutionary and comprehensive piece of child care legislation that would mount the platform by pronouncing new and extended measures and powers. This also reinforced the role of courts in child care proceedings. More pointedly, this empowered social workers (for those with a primary responsibility of child protection and investigations) with what they had been lacking for many years. Correspondingly, the rise of children going into residential care gave credence for additional legislation. In recognition of this, the 1989 act also devoted sections relevant to the monitoring and regulation of children in residential sectors. These regulations comprise part of the children act 1989 and are enshrined in volume 4 covering children residential sectors. With the increase of children going into care of the local authorities during the 1990s, this influx increased the demand to regulate residential sectors more closely, not to mention introduce additional procedures and legislation. These were elevated with the *National Minimum Standards, the Care Standards Act 2000*[12] and the *Children's Home Regulation 2001*[13]. It was of no consequence that the concept of significant harm has rapidly evolved. This would give entrance to other imperative childcare enactments. Some of these have been ratified with the following; Adoption and Children Act 2002, Carers and Disabled Act 2000 and Children and Adoption Act 2006.

On this point, social workers had been given reinforcements. Now armed with substantial and extended 'legal ammunition' social workers were deployed at the frontline to mobilise the act's key priorities in accordance with s*(1)*, '*the welfare of the child is paramount*'[14] with extreme prejudice. The first and most obvious target, which we has been clear from the outset, was to eliminate or minimise any 'risks' or 'harm' that threatened the child and in this sense, our interest lies with unimpeachable authenticity of the 'welfare of children and young people' This point has now become a dominant factor over the decades,

---

12   The Care Standards Act 2000.

13   The Children's Homes Regulations 2001.

14   The Children Act 1989.

not just within social work but other disciplines, sectors and professions, especially were a key component of their work is focused on engaging with children and young people. In fact, the welfare principle has also been elevated with numerous quotations from those employed in disciplines such as education, youth work, youth justice and camhs and further transcending anywhere where children and young people are integral to the service provided. The constant abuse of children and young people began to dominate agendas. To wit, this gave the welfare factor more authority, especially having the weight of government backing to enforce its position to safeguard their interests without reservation or invitation. Having now acquired a national and international recognition and prestige, it would eventually transmit itself into a range of paradigmatic settings, especially where the dangers of extremism have begun to surface.

Alongside this, the Act compelled professionals to admonish the '*wishes and feelings*' of children to be seriously taken into consideration. This ensured that a child-centred approach was core to the process, and that any outcome would have to be in the vetted interest of the child both in the short and long term. Continuing with its vision, and remaining faithful to its original intention, the amendment of the Children Act in 2004 extended these provisions. To help stabilise this, new administrations in the form of Local Children's Safeguarding Boards were introduced replacing the previous Area Child Protection Committees from 1974. The 2004 act legislated that all local authorities must make provisions to safeguard children within their respective jurisdiction and to collaborate with agencies where matters of safeguarding were of significance in accordance with applicable protocols and procedures. This updated legislation advocated and highlighted that inter-agency working in particular, was a critical juncture in the process and towards providing some securitisation. The terrorist attacks in 2005 would widen their scope in this sense. It is here, that these attacks tested these boards' ability to adjust to these safeguarding complexities presented within these new realms. It could be argued, that all these imperative measures gave the impression that all danger to children and young people welfare were now well covered; this was in danger of leading to a growing laxity from professionals. The terrorist attacks in 2005 reminded us otherwise. It was obvious, that swift responses were required to safeguard children and young people from extremism. Initially, these proposals seemed outlandish by reason of their lack of pre-existence in practice and were in danger of being misunderstood as anecdotal.

In spite of this, this drove forward attainment influencing a series of consultations and topical discussion, especially between children's services and counter-terrorism departments, with a view to thrash out key concerns. These discussions also sought to expound upon distinct terms such as significant harm and required some consolidation outside of its conventional setting largely situated within a social care context. Those responsible engaged in multiple processes and transactions with the intention to establish a template that revolved around safeguarding vulnerable children and young people from extremism, many who were vulnerable by virtue of their immaturity and dependency on others. This generated a tremendous sense of expectation. However, this venture was running the risk of a backlash. This, both as a notion and concept, was uncharted territory for any service to expound upon and was a risky venture, and any failure of social services to protect children and young people from extremism was likely to put them back on trial. It was predicted that casualties would emerge and given these concerns resulted in safeguarding and Prevent publications.

These proposals were not without their farcical moments. Those who were religiously devout to their profession and with a vested interest to safeguard became susceptible to counter-terrorism agendas, lacking the credentials, depending on others to provide some scholarship. This dependency hindered their progress. This was perplexing. One of the problems here of course, was that such matters had not been thoroughly explored prior to the London bombings. Discussions in political and security realms, on the other hand, were thriving, primarily triggered by the terrorist attacks in New York on September 11th 2001. The 'war on terror' so termed by the Bush administration, compelled British security services such as MI5 and MI6 to engage in numerous high profile board room discussions, concerning the security of the British public. Of course, aspects of these discussions focused on the repercussion of Britain engaging in the war in Iraq and the rise of radicalisation in the UK particularly amongst Muslim youth. An increase of resources and manpower were necessary to prevent any unexpected consequences or invitations. The informing and mobilising process, in terms of prevention, would eventually be executed through the government's Contest strategy. This has become the government's preferred counter-terrorism response for all front-line services and organisations, especially those working with children and young people. Additionally, the acquisition of terrorism legislation would forewarn many, coming to the rescue of vulnerable individuals. Given these new legislative powers, the Crown Prosecution Service (CPS) would eventually delight themselves with an abundance of promising convictions. Prior to the terrorist attacks in 2005, the responsibility to safeguard children and young people from the threat of terrorism fell extensively into the hands of security services and the British government. This has gradually changed post 7/7, incorporating a wider taskforce.

In backtracking slightly to incorporate other imperatives, efforts to protect the welfare of children were accelerated, according to section 17 of the Children Act in terms of defining a 'child in need'. These culminated with the creation of another HM Government publication through The Department of Health (DoH) entitled *Assessment Framework Model implemented in 2000*[15].This was issued under section 7 of the Local Authority Act 1970. This framework enabled professionals a more '*systematic way of analysing, and understanding what is happening to children and young people*.' This covered three distinct categories that incorporated the following; *parenting capacity, child's development, family and environmental factors.* The purpose of the documentation was to '*understand the child's need within the family context*' by keeping the focus on the child. This publication was on at least some good ground and the appeal of the document gave positive scope. However, this depended heavily on the professional judgement of its workers to critically discern the degree of harm envisaged to the child within these highly charged social environments. These long-standing difficulties, pertaining to the quality of judgements, have become embedded in governmental publications that have repeatedly stressed, in terms of responsibility, '*it is left at the discretion of the professional to determine what constitutes significant harm*'[16]. Indeed, it is precisely because of these observational judgements, that both the reliability and credibility of professionals, have been brought into serious question. These judgements intending to act as a beneficiary could either obstruct the process or at the same time steer this in preferred directions. These observations are well documented by Milner and O'Bryan, '*social workers are asked to make judgements about what is good enough for meeting children safety and well-being*'. By reason of the Children Act 1989 defining a child in need and at risk brought with it its own complexities, and the terrorist attacks in 2005 have certainly taken this to new heights of meaning, let alone complexity. A continuation of safeguarding failures has given credence to further governmental reforms. It is disturbing to know that since 1948 there have been an estimated 70 public inquiries into child abuse cases and the fact that 80 children die each year from cases of abuse and neglect is alarming - according to reports these figures

---

15   The Children Act 1989.

16   Working Together to Safeguard Children - HM Government 2006.

have remained consistent over the years[17]

The Lord Laming inquiry in 2003 (due to death of Victoria Climbié aged 8 years old in 2000) offloaded numerous imperatives complied in the form of a operational document entitled the 'green paper' At the same time, it initiated one of the first joint chief inspection report on safeguarding children (2002) which unsurprisingly, highlighted the lack of priority status given to safeguarding. In sum, in his 2003 report to the government on the death of Victoria Climbié, Lord Laming stated,

'I recognise that those who take on the work of protecting children at risk of deliberate harm face a tough and challenging task... Adults who deliberately exploit the vulnerability of children can behave in devious and menacing ways. They will often go to great lengths to hide their activities from those concerned for the well-being of a child...(child protection) staff have to balance the rights of a parent with that of the protection of the child' (Lord Laming 2003:3).

Lord Laming reinforces this message in his 2009 progress report on child protection for the government

The authorial intent of Lord Laming's report gave credence to the inception of another government initiative in 2003. The 'Every Child Matters'[18] was a codified response that sought to regulate matters. This landmark framework, often called a 'sea change' to the children and families agenda, partly introduced due to Victoria's death, sought to mediate by addressing the needs of children and young people, with the explicit intention to thrust forward and promote multi-agency working, by supporting and encouraging children and young people to meet the goals specified in the framework. Principally, it would cover the following categories; 'Being healthy', 'staying safe', 'Enjoy and achieve' 'Making a positive contribution' and 'Economic well-being' Of course, because of these obligations and in regards to the safeguarding of children and young people compliance would become statutory. The backing from articles of the United Nations Conventions, less shy about their role, enforced this point through prescribed international directives and treaties. In exercising their authority, reminded governments that they were admonished to vocalise these protocols, particularly in reference to aspects that demanded in these protocols that *'Children and young people are safe from maltreatment, neglect, violence and sexual exploitation'*[19]. These protocols were also assigned

---

17   HC Deb, 23 January 2003, col 738 (Alan Milburn MP, Secretary of State, Commons Statement on the Victoria Climbié Report).

18   Every Child Matters .

19   Every Child Matters (Five Outcomes) United Nations Convention on the Rights of the Child (UNCRC) (UNICEF).

to inform professionals to be extra diligent and cautious whilst on social patrol to 'look out' for any dangers that threatened the welfare of children and young people. The ECM concepts and framework have become familiar to most child-centred services in the UK and have been absorbed into various policies, systems, protocols and procedures within statutory, voluntary, charitable and private organisations, and have become an active agents ever since. Equally as important contingency planning was vital to ensure consistency and sustainability. This initiative was the start of another long-winded process and it was envisaged that further publications and reviews were warranted to monitor these and other concerns. These additional publications focused their efforts towards strengthening communication between agencies and early intervention, as a result of the aforementioned concerns.

A post inquiry conducted by Lord Laming in 2004 resulted in another HM publication in 2006. This inquiry was in joint collaboration with the Department of Health and entitled 'what to do if you're worried a child is being abused' The information that was contained, encouraged dialogue by prompting and compelling agencies to make use of the safeguarding content and by making this more digestible for professionals to transmit within their daily administrations, enabled many to focus their attention on delivery and strengthened communication between agencies. This orientation led many towards embracing this publication's recommendations with aspects that were key to this success in terms of inter-agency working and taking appropriate action to safeguard and to promote children welfare, which saw many learn valuable lessons from the death of Victoria in 2003. This was so desperately required; ensuring children safety, welfare and protection were both prioritised and maximised. However, and like always, this invited further internal changes, reforms and challenges.

In terms of accommodating these proposed transitions, and to state the obvious, for any reforms to be firstly, introduced and then secondly, implemented could not be done overnight. Delays are often inevitable. It has been a common trend, that due to these long-winded processes, those delays have often been the culprit that has been held responsible for creating internal problems and places the child at an administrative risk and disadvantage. These delays gave oxygen to fuel frustrations. Again, we are informed by the Children Act that *delays must be avoided*[20] The daunting task to find concrete solutions to resolve this epidemic and to protect children is a problem that continues to repeat itself time and time again. This has been

---

20   Children Act 1989 s1(2).

apparent with the most recent review of child protection systems in 2011, conducted by Professor Monroe, stemming from a highly charged social work setting. There were lessons to be learnt from this review, which are discussed in more detail in chapter five. As predicted, the strenuous efforts of many social workers took its toll. These systems immobilised many, causing some to work on overdrive, especially to address the backlog of cases that had already existed. This confined many to administrative roles. This did not look promising for what was on the horizon, given that any practical approaches to safeguard children and young people cannot be done effectively from behind a desk or with a computer that fails to discern danger! It is here that I postulate, it was not a question of 'if' children and young people would engage in violent extremism or terrorism, but a question of 'when'. These dire prophecies eventually came true and the task to ensure the safety of children and young people had been taken to another climax. However, prior to the July 7th terrorist attacks, we have well established that draconian measures had already taken formation through various reforms, reviews, legislation and publication introduced and certainly, after the events in 2005, these have become more active.

As we have briefly touched upon earlier, we are informed that according to the Children Act 2004, especially in respect to section 14 (1), that each Local Authority must establish a Local Safeguarding Children Board that has a primary function on promoting the welfare of children and young people. It would be these LSCB that would became the responsible agents, after 7/7, which would provide and transport a range of safeguarding materials to crossover into counter-terrorism work and landscapes conflating these in the process. This comprised of providing the appropriate procedures, templates, assessments formats and criteria's and systems that were drastically needed to establish and to maintain this new alliance and towards preserving its co-existence. This is expounded upon in chapter four. This embellishment embodied what the *Working together to Safeguard Children* document had previously stipulated as a *'shared responsibility and the need for effective joint working between agencies and professionals that have different roles and expertise'[21]*. From this premise, this did not alter the social workers' duty to respond, in any way, shape or form, on the reverse, gave credence for insight on an rapidly developing and international agenda. This had an irreversible impact across a wide range of social and child-centred stratas and set the stage for greater exposure.

---

21 HM Government Working together to Safeguard Children (A guide to inter-agency working to safeguard and promote the welfare to children).

The terrorist attacks in London opened the room for further discussion. Involved in these discussions, again, would be the Department of Health (DoH). This discussion drove the DoH towards addressing the wider risks of extremism and radicalisation and towards securing the safety of vulnerable individuals. In this sense, as it did previously with the Assessment Framework Model in 2000 with children, documents emerged. Its contributions towards preventing violent extremism would be seen in 2011 in the form of a document entitled, *Building Partnerships, Staying Safe - The Healthcare Sector's contribution to HM Government's Prevent Strategy: for healthcare organisations*. In short, aspects of the document stipulated that the significance of inter-agency working was a crucial factor in the fight against extremism and the risk of radicalisation of vulnerable individuals in this sense, were directed to vulnerable patients. This is a point expounded upon in chapter five. Resultantly, we can clearly see here the proselytising role of Prevent, has begun to pervade and was somewhat becoming monolithic as a result. The terrorist attacks in 2005 could not transpire at a more critical and transitional time, especially in light of the aforementioned changes to current safeguarding reforms, publications and legislation, which, controversially, some that have been conceived at the expense of 'failure within the system' to protect vulnerable children; this did not look promising. This has left a very staggering picture. The dependency on the state to respond to these extremism concerns was drastically needed. Since 7/7, this has certainly demanded 'all hands on deck' especially in terms of safeguarding the welfare of children and young people, child protection, prevention and early intervention.

SAFEGUARDING FROM EXTREMISM

The London Bombings in July 2005 was devastating. Four British born men detonated a series of bombs in London killing 52 people and injuring several hundred. The immediate impact was felt by those living in the UK and, given the terrorist attacks in America on September 11th 2001 a few years earlier, certainly opened past wounds and inflicted new ones. Shock exemplified the reaction as millions watched in disbelief at the horrific events unfolding in London that day. No more persuasion was needed. In less than a few hours the extent of damage caused by these British terrorists would re-arrange the perceptions of the British public and many terrorism experts. What many experts had already anticipated, having observed 9/11, had repeated itself on July 7th 2005. The iconic imagery of a destroyed London bus, not only instilled a sense of anxiety, but also ignited a painful dissection and self-examination of societal infrastructures that existed in the UK. It was the notion of 'home-grown terrorism' that is and has frightened many. The origins were obvious.

Terrorist groups had recruited and radicalised those living within the UK to execute horrific acts of suicide bombings, often prolific in countries such as Iran, Afghanistan and Syria. It was even more painful to accept, that these extremists, notably, were of 'British origin'. This has created unrest in the UK. What was equally frightening, having already experienced 7/7, was the unforeseen danger that was on the horizon. This surrounded the grooming and recruitment of children and young people by extremists. This surprisingly caught many off guard. It was clear that terrorism had taken mainstream safeguarding by surprise. In responding, the government 'rolled up their sleeves' in efforts to tackle this emerging epidemic. The need to protect from this 'disease' would become a critical factor, not just in safeguarding terms but in preventing the 'toxicology of extremism' from spreading within the UK. In my view the pain staking efforts of extremists to 'spread such a disease' through recruiting children and young people could be expected to continue for many years to come. On this point, it introduces other approaches that have tenable relevance to this subject, especially in preventing violence from spreading. A leading expert on epidemics, Dr Gary Sultken, has provided some insight that may prove useful towards preventing violent extremism. He has applied a popular concept which he has referred to as 'how to reverse an epidemic' towards addressing the wider problems of violent behaviour. Within this context he stress that by 'understanding how violence spreads' will educate and inform us on a range of ways of applying prevention approaches in efforts to stop or prevent violent growth patterns. He argues, fundamentally, that there are three stages that can stop an epidemic from spreading, even if they are humans that are spreading this 'violent disease'. He has outlined these in the following stages. Firstly 'Interrupting Transmission, secondly, 'Prevent Future Spread' and thirdly, 'Shifting the Norms'. It is worth storing these points in mind, for further consideration in prevention terms.

The response to these attacks would initially be the form of a strategic counter-terrorism measure developed by the Home Office in 2003 called CONTEST[22]. With many strands of operation to this counter-terrorism document, it quickly acquired a reputation that has also managed to transform many services and organisations delivering preventative work. The strategy described its key features in the form of; Pursue, Protect, Prepare and Prevent, with the Prevent strand being the most applicable to many

---

22   Home Office website - Government 'Contest Strategy'.

frontline professionals and organisations, especially those services working with children and young people. The remaining three strands Pursue, Prepare and Protect, would be applicable to security, intelligence and law enforcement agencies, though some overlap would be inevitable. Prevent has acquired a growing reputation and is defined in the current counter-terrorism strategy as,

'The purpose of Prevent is to stop people from becoming or supporting terrorism. This includes countering terrorist ideology and challenging those who promote it; supporting individuals who are especially vulnerable to becoming radicalised; and working with sectors and institutions where the risk of radicalisation is assessed to be high'[23]

Prevent, launched in the wake of the July 7th London bombings significantly instructed many regarding measures for 'preventing violent extremism'. This was not as straightforward as envisaged. Many professionals lacked the credentials to work on terrorism agendas, let alone deliver assessment or models of intervention that were geared towards addressing extremism, many depending extensively on their formal training acquired elsewhere in attempts to provide some solutions. Some of these prerequisites derived from curriculum-based academic programmes. Adaptions were necessary. While their formal and academic training empowered many to translate a wide range of skills and knowledge into a range of social environments, this provided very little scope in attempting to answer or respond to the many contentious questions unpacked from this new agenda. For example, what type of assessment would be applicable? defining extremism? identifying signs of radicalisation and referral processes? Undoubtedly, more was needed to help. Troubling signs emerged.

Raising the profile of extremism, purely from a social work context with a view to develop and conduct assessments and interventions, was initially, complex and un-codified. A sharper focus was needed. Nonetheless, despite these voids, the threats from extremists who pledged to randomly recruit children and young people in the UK overrode the lack of preparation, which in the eyes of security services such MI5 and Home Office, could not be prolonged, having already informed us that extremists sought to advance their *'religious and ideological agendas'* within the UK. These fears triggered a series of consultations, the aim being, for those working with children and young people to make radical organisational adjustments and to equip professionals with what they needed to work within a terrorism context. These consisted with some of the following reviewing practices, policies and

23   The Home Office, the four Ps– Prevent, Pursue, Protect and Prepare 2011.

procedures and to enrol many into counter-terrorism training programmes. This accelerated many towards implementing preventative measures to deter vulnerable children and young people from extremism, as the anticipation of another terrorist attack lingered. The disenchantment of extremists has escalated these threats. These have been in tangible form, in that they have continued to 'take the fight' to security services, which is repeatedly seen in their constant motivations to recruit individuals irrespective of their location. This was apparent post 7/7 and the list of suspects began to emerge including both young and old.

FROM SUSPICIONS TO SUSPECTS

In 2006, Hammad Munshi would become the youngest person to date to be convicted of terrorism in the UK. Police had found materials in the form of a guide to death and explosives in his bedroom; he also possessed notes on martyrdom under his bed. Munshi, whose grandfather is a leading Islamic scholar, was 15 and taking his GCSEs when arrested. Leeds's counter-terrorism unit began an arrest after suspicions arose. The Judge, Timothy Pontius, remanded Munshi in custody at the time. The CPS said that Munshi at the time was the youngest person to be convicted under the Terrorism Act. Munshi's radicalisation was a result of 23 year old Adbid Khan who was said to be central in radicalising people. The court had heard that Munshi spent hours surfing jihadist websites and distributing material to others as part of what the prosecution branded a 'worldwide conspiracy' to wipe out 'non-Muslims'. The material contained detailed instructions about making napalm, other high explosives, detonators and grenades, plus, 'how to kill' instructions.

Munshi also possessed an on-line Arabic profile 'fidadee' - meaning a 'person ready to sacrifice themselves for a particular cause' – ran a website selling hunting knives and Islamic flags and was the cell's computer specialist; he also had Al-Qaeda propaganda videos and recordings on his PC, promoting 'murder and destruction'. Munshi also admitted to being interested in jihad as a 12 year old. The jury convicted Munshi along with co-conspirators, on eight Terrorism Act offences committed between November 23rd 2005 and June 20th 2006. Detective Chief Superintendent John Parkinson, head of CTU, after the case, described the defendants as 'dangerous individuals' who were in possession of material that was useful to anyone wanting to commit an act of terrorism. In terms of statutory obligations to disclose, the Terrorism Act 2000 makes it a criminal offence for a person to fail to disclose, without reasonable excuse, any information which he either knows or believes might help prevent another person carrying out an act of terrorism or might help in bringing a terrorist to justice in the UK, even if this may be a young person, given its clauses. His interest in jihad at the age of 12 years old would automatically signify a safeguarding problem.

The list would extend. In 2008, the conversion of a young white male, called Nicky Riley, demonstrated to us the power that distorted versions of religion have on the vulnerable. His conversion to a radical version of Islam culminated in him changing his name to Mohammed Abdullah Azeem. This also accelerated the process and, with other medical factors at play, contributed to his radicalisation. This led to his failed attempt to blow up the Giraffe restaurant in Exeter during May 2008. It was later established that he had been recruited through social media. What was frightening in this case, was those religious extremist that were held responsible for his radicalisation, had recruited him without even having met with him in person. It was clear that Nicky was the target of extremist whose grievances against the UK, sought to take revenge by using their own British people to wage a war against their own country. This was a clear indication that extremist had very little respect for any person, irrespective of their race, religion or origin . This dichotomous relationship would seem to have found its legitimised manifestation, in meeting extremist expectations, chiefly, to incite fear, cause major disruption and magnify Islam in the eyes of 'unbelievers'. Riley had previously been diagnosed with an inherent autistic spectrum condition aged 9, which immobilised his cognitive ability to discern any unforeseen dangers. His regular contact with mental health professionals, where he would often discuss issues of terrorism with them, was an opportunity to intervene with scope for further assessments to take place. This was a clear sign and indication that his ideology was imported from somewhere. He would later be convicted of terrorism related offences and sentenced to 8 years in prison. The following year in 2009, Andrew Ibrahim was jailed in 2009 for plotting to blow up a shopping centre in Bristol and in December 2010, Tamiour Abdulwahab al-Abdaly killed himself in a bomb attack in Stockholm, Sweden. His extreme beliefs and behaviours raised concerns having attended a mosque in Luton, UK. These cases highlights the consequences of not responding on time, particularly to those vulnerable individuals; this point would be echoed in the Prevent agenda, in so far as much, *'These and other cases demonstrate the consequences for failures to intervene at key times during their radicalisation'*[24]. The traces of safeguarding failures can be seen throughout. The problems of Islamist extremism and the rise of

---

24 The HM Prevent agenda (2011).

the far-right, have presented considerable problems for social work professionals, especially in terms of child protection, post 7/7.

In one case, social workers from Durham County Council sought to take an unborn child from its devoted mother. Concerns arose around a 25 year old mother, who had previously attended EDL marches, with a string of offences including attacking police during a 2010 EDL march, and was known as the 'English Angel'. It was decided that due to such extreme views associated with the EDL that risks to the unborn child could affect the baby's welfare. Social workers feared that the child would be radicalised with EDL views and had put up the child for adoption. Controversy arose when extreme radicals such as Islamic cleric Abu Qatada's children would still remain in his care. Given this comparison, the Liberal Democrat MP John Hemming would raise this in the House of Commons, to address the imbalance of this case. In another instance, a girl was dressed in a hat stating *'I love Al-Qaeda'* by her parents for a 2006 London protest, providing some evidence, that children as young as four could be monitored by terror police who believe they could be brainwashed by Islamic extremists. It is therefore necessary that we must go deeper still, especially towards gaining a comprehensive understanding of extremism.

EXTREMISM – DEFINITION AND CONTEXT

'Extremism' a notoriously ambiguous word, requires some consolidation, especially for the growing number of professionals entering the agenda. I shall set a context for the reader that is integral to this research, given that the notorious actions of extremists cannot be thoroughly understood without establishing some clear points. By this we shall briefly explore, defining extremism, comprehending it terms and agreeing some objectives. I must remind the readers, that my definition of extremism discussed from this chapter onwards is one that incorporates motivations that are driven by an ideology that has an intention to use violence or terrorism as a means of fulfilling its objective and persuading others to follow suit. I must also remind the readers that the use of terms disused in this material may have some similarities and overlap, for example, 'extremist', 'radical' and 'terrorist'. For the purpose of this study, it is the actions of extremists that we are concerned about and where their extreme views can lead towards acts of full blown terrorism, towards supporting the use of terrorism or encouraging towards violence. Some of the terms that will be used will have some cross-over, for example, extremist and violent extremist. I will attempt to provide clear examples and illustrations when using these terms. These are expounded further in chapter three, though some context is required here.

In terms of state responses to extremism, this has generated a tremendous sense of expectation. The current Prevent agenda has stipulated that any response to extremism, without the expressed use of violence, will be dealt with by CLG (Communities Local Government); on the other hand, extremism which promotes the use of violence and that is driven towards terrorism or terrorism related activity will be the responsibility of Prevent. On this point, extremism is defined within the current Prevent agenda as *'a vocal or active opposition to fundamental British values, including democracy, the rule of law, individual liberty and mutual respect and tolerance of different faiths and beliefs. Also included in extremism are calls for the death of members of the armed forces, whether in this country or overseas[25]'* On this point, extremism or harboring extreme views that promotes the use of violence, even if they are against British values must be considered dangerous and in this sense, is a threat to any democratic order. Research also suggests that, *'extremism is a psychological phenomenon that can be broken down into several causes. It is important to understand this when dealing with it, and in order to keep our own thoughts and feelings moderate and rational[26]*. We can therefore agree that in this phenomenon, some people are more vulnerable to extreme views than others and in this sense children and young people are particularly vulnerable. Others have suggested that extremism is highly dangerous because it often results in views that are *'detached from reality'* and which are also destructive to the ideals of others. In this same view, I propose that the *'self-deception of violent extremists may reduce their ability to see themselves as others do'*. In this sense, extremists sought to open another dispensation. Some of these views may be unpopular but are necessary for this study. It is with these views that we intend to progress.

Not surprisingly then, the waves of admission have stretched some beyond reasoning and rationality. For example, religious extremists in particular, have routinely held unrealistic positions that are exclusively pertaining to God and as a consequence, have detached themselves from reality in the process. Because of these pneumatological reasons, the heights that extremists have set are 'out of range' having conscientiously elected themselves to become 'judge, jury and executioners'. Because of this, they have completely detached themselves from any logical reasoning. By self-proclaiming to be the advocates of God, they have retaliated and unequivocally challenged the 'status quo'. It is in the same line of reasoning that I postulate, that extremists have also attempted

---

25 Government Prevent agenda.
26 Community Care, 2014.

to provide some 'scholarship' appealing to others to join in their quests for ultimate liberation. This needs strong protest. This is clearly apparent within video footage released before and after terror attacks or incidents, that have constantly discredited western governments. It was also clear that extremists sought to force the public to tolerate their presence. Other negative examples are exemplified in their social behaviour.

Their violent expressions and blatant disregard to uphold British values have clearly brought them into disfavour with governments and it was clear that no more could be tolerated, and if they did not abandon their ways, harsh action would follow. This has been clearly demonstrated by British governments that have contended with their 'unrealistic demands' and 'far-fetched view' by prohibiting laws and values that are incompatible with British values to be implemented within the UK - Sharia Law being one. On this point, the Home Secretary, Theresa May, has warned of the dangers of Sharia courts operating in Britain which do not work in the interest of 'British values'. Other governmental offensives were delivered through legislation. It is terrorist threats that have created new terrorism laws.

The introduction of terrorism legislation within the UK was a robust response. Commissioned by the conservative government during 1996 and led by Lord Lloyd of Berwick a serving law lord, the Inquiry into *Legislation against Terrorism* issued a two-volume report in 1996. In short, his recommendations proposed that a permanent anti-terrorism legislation that reflected changes in terrorism globally needed to be considered. This transformation was completed by the Blair administration with the formalisation of the Terrorism Act 2000. Once enacted, it broadened the definition of terrorism, repealing the previous Act from 1974. The 2000 Act also constrained terrorist groups from expressing their 'extreme views' in the public domain, particularly those that had the sole intention and purpose to advocate violence or the threat of the use of violence as integral to their advancement. These actions were contrary to the Terrorism Act 2000 by reason of *section (1)* '*the use of threat ....for the purpose of advancing a political, religious or ideological cause*'[27] making this a criminal offence within the UK. In tightening its grip further, the introduction of additional legislation was seen with the Terrorism Acts 2005 and 2006. These sought to regulate terrorism activity by introducing the use of control orders and reprimanding anyone that glorified acts or anything related to magnifying terrorism. These extensions incorporated those that had alleged ties to groups operating or financing terrorism outside of the UK and

---

27   Terrorism Act 2000 s(1)(2).

fell into definitions such as, *'supply of finances, supplying materials and dissemi-nating materials and publications'*[28] - this was a step in the right direction in securing all routes. However, in spite of the persuading power of legislation, which could at best only arrest those suspected or caught red-handed in acts of terrorism; a more pragmatic approach was needed for those working at the frontline. This would enable many to counter the rapidly growing concerns that comprise the complexities surrounding the 'grooming' 'recruitment' and the 'radicalisation' of vulnerable children and young people, before any legal intervention. A further development is more recent in the legal spheres.

New proposals announced by the Home Secretary Theresa May, in 2015, were delivered in the form of range of measures to prevent extremism including the exclusive use of 'Extremist Disruption Orders'. This was certainly sugges-tive that the increase and use of law enforcement was the only option avail-able to dismantle extremism. Similarities of this type of response to problem-atic behaviour were seen from 1997. The previous Labour Prime Minister, Tony Blair, with his popular 'zero tolerance approach' which was applied towards addressing the growing problems of anti-social behaviour during the earlier period of 2000. These diverse problems gave credence to intro-duce the 'Anti-Social Behaviour Act 2003'. Professor Clive Walker, a leading authority on terrorism legislation, has argued similarly, that legal responses to the complexities and reasons behind terrorist attacks are the evidence of a *'traumatised polity'*[29]. More pointedly, Walker refers to use of the term 'zero tolerance' in referring to the current concerns of the Charity Commission's slow progress to deploy counter-terrorism measures-such as Prevent-against known organisations that have been suspected of financing terrorism, with some trustees of these trusted organisations having alleged links to terrorist groups such as Al-Qaeda. In his submission to the House of Commons Home Affairs Committee, Professor Walker stressed that, *'the commission was slow to use its powers to tackle suspect abuse of charities by terrorists'.* He said that the commission's track record *'does not match the seriousness with which the threat of terrorism is depicted within Contest'* - the government's counter-terrorism strategy. *'It is not the case that the commission ignores allegations of terrorism,'* he said. *'Rather, the issue is whether its resolve to deal with the allegations is sufficiently firm.'*

At best, legislation lacked the tenacity to examine the wider 'social and

---

28   The Terrorism Act 2001, 2005 and 2006.

29   Cyber-Terrorism: Legal principle and law in the United Kingdom, page 625, Professor Clive Walker (ethics of responding to terrorism).

psychological' dimensions or constructs. These involved examining aspects such as distorted thinking, identity crisis and a range of medical conditions as precursors to a person overall engagement in extremism. It was not good enough just to establish 'intent' which for legal purposes had considerable advantage. Having identified these complexities, a range of publications, theoretical frameworks and research came to the rescue and were also geared towards focusing on and examining the microscopic dimension of abuse as a form of maltreatment within this new context, which was largely overlooked. I must stress here, that these dimensions could take form in what many professionals have become accustomed to in safeguarding terms as incorporating anyone of the key criteria covering; 'physical, sexual, emotional or neglect'. These cannot be covered in detail in this chapter or material and would require a whole new dominance. What is even more important here, however, is that this could provide further insight that could help to explain the adverse effects that were responsible for causing the emotional and psychological traumas resulting from the direct engagement because of extremism, which in this sense, are better understood from a perspective that would describe the dangers this would present to children and young people exposed to extremism material or environments. In terms of abuse, these could be linked to 'feelings of distress, being frightened or frequent bullying'. This has some substance, especially in terms of establishing trigger points whilst exposed to these dangers. It is here that these dynamics are both open to discussion and to be considered within this agenda and given what has already been suggested from parliamentary rhetoric on these issues, is left at the discretion of professionals to take lead responsibilities to commence social proceedings to investigate these matters of abuse further.

Given this view, The House of Commons Education Committee fourth report and session 2012-13, *Children first: the child protection system in England* of the Munro Review with reference to conduct inquiry 6 has stressed to '*identify children at risk of different forms of abuse and exploitation including and but not restricted to child trafficking, on-line.*' Not surprisingly then, Professor Munro, has summed up this complex challenge, '*it is not enough to identify abuse or neglect. Signs and symptoms are often ambiguous.*'[30] Taking these views into account, this embryonic shift within this new extremism context, however, is interesting, yet, scary, as it continues to evolve. This then has wider implications in practice and research. On this point, we must also conform to the line of reasoning presented by a leading expert, Professor Majed Ashy an assistant professor of psychology

30 The Monroe Review, 2011.

at Merrimack College and a research fellow in psychiatry at the Developmental Bio-psychiatry Research Program at McLean Hospital, at Harvard Medical School, USA. His research on the subject of 'child abuse and extremism' attempt to shed light on this point. In a recent interview, he informs us that the limbic system functionality, the part of the brain associated with emotions, is strongly correlated to childhood abuse. When the limbic system does not develop properly as a result of physical or emotional abuse, children grow up to have emotional and physical problems. Professor Ashy explains that a child's brain tries to adjust to the circumstances it finds itself in within the limits of its genetic structure. As a result, in harsh abusive environments, a child's brain can develop in to dysfunction. This led Professor Ashy to consider whether extremism was biologically based in the brain.

EXTREMISM, RESILIENCE AND RESPONSES

We are accustomed with extensive research that suggests traumas will have major impact on children's and young people's development, which for the extremist intending to recruit vulnerable individuals might have major gains. Contributions from figures such as Jean Pigate (child development) Howard Gardern (intelligence) Daniel Goleman (emotional intelligence) and Erik Erikson (psycho-social development) have philosophical and ontological importance towards explaining key stages and transitions that could open these vulnerabilities and which is where we need to revive some of these in order to prevent any risks or threats and to focus our attention on early intervention. If we accept their concepts and fundamental principles, which I presume, many of us have, myself included, this may provide key messages to help build resilience in children and young people, especially during early childhood.

For example, Howard Gardern research on 'intra-personal intelligence' 31 which he conducted during the early 1980s, and was further developed by Daniel Goleman during the 1990', fundamentally explains the processes and components that build, what most professional working with children and young people have become accustomed to know as 'emotional intelligence' which for the purpose of providing and supplying protective factors for children and young people to guard against dangers to their self, has some good ground. He stresses that, '*emotional intelligence is the ability to understand and use your own feelings to help cope with issues in life.*'[31] It is during the early stages of a child's life that the quality of an intervention that is employed

31   Health and Social care, Neil Moonie, 2004, page 258.

will determine whether these mechanism are or have been installed, which again fall extensively into the hands of the worker and their ability to critically discern the need for these mechanism to be learnt, which may not be visible at the time. This will help to set boundaries and install sanctions for the purpose of prevention, especially towards steering them away in the short and long-term from negative influences. It is in these instances that our hypothesis is tested then validated. In these preliminary efforts, the intention of deploying and installing coping mechanisms during these developmental stages, may or will disrupt the route that extremists use to indoctrinate them. This clearly illustrates at least one fundamental point out of many, without these instal-ments a child with minimal coping mechanisms, low level emotional intel-ligence and lack of protective factors, can vocalise, as stressed in our opening chapter, *'when I grow up I want to be a terrorist'*. It is here, that our visibility is a lot clearer. This raises further questions.

For example, if the threat imposed by extremists is intended to cause some adverse effects then this must conclude or incorporate the child experiencing some form of 'present or immediate harm or danger'. It is here that we both reflect and speculate, that a child in the care of any individual harbouring extreme views that are of a violent nature or loaded with violent connota-tions, would give us some indication that the child's welfare will more than likely result in them experiencing some form of harm or even trauma. This has critical importance and where we must occupy ourselves by exploring these issues further. Whereas, on the other hand, children or young people who advance their extreme views, irrespective of the location or environ-ment are liable for the damaged caused. For example, the use of inappropriate and offensive linguistics such as 'shouting jihad' or 'all Christians or Jew are devils' assures us, that these have the potential to transform, create or turn into violent behaviour at the expense of opposing individuals. It is here that those extremists are delighted with these results, having demonstrated these points themselves. For the many professionals, this is disturbing.

The way that extremists influence children and young people towards engaging in violence has been striking. The tactics used to steer children and young people towards these realms has been subtle. Extremist having imposed complex and dangerous views upon children and young people is disturbing and cause for alarm. The negative connotations contained in these extreme views are evident of these disturbances. Again, reminding the readers of my point that extremists are attempting to provide some 'scholarship' to the vulnerable, irrespective if this endangers them, this needs strong protest. This is certainly suggestive that the degree of harm pertaining to children is raised dramatically, given the exposure and territory in which children and young people encounter extremism, can be exciting, yet, taxing. This brings back to our attention to discuss an HM Government document entitled *Working together to safeguard children, a guide to inter-agency working to safeguard and promote the welfare of children - every child matters*. This publication sought to expound on this type of maltreatment that is inflicted because of the degree of harm exposed to the individual has become more diverse and threatening, in our case it is diverse because of its exposure to violent extremism. The document informs us that *'abuse and neglect are forms of maltreatment, and may abuse or neglect a child by inflicting harm by failing to act to prevent harm'*[32] - this may come from family members or even strangers. In efforts to raise the profile of abuse, the severity of the matter would be showcased in a BBC report in 2014 informing us that *'Psychological abuse should be made a crime'* suggesting criminal sanctions to become applicable. It is this type of psychological abuse that is inflicted because of the exposure to dangerous views of extremists and that needs to be discerned by professionals, where our research interest lies and where further research by experts is seriously required. Points I have raised at times during practice. It is also in the same breath that I postulate, that in doing so, this could prevent extremists from recruiting in a number of ways. This can include by importing or applying sanctions that are geared towards protecting children and young people, which is also intended to prevent the perpetrator from repeating this type of behaviour. This has positive connotations for developing research that is focused towards safeguarding from extremism. Next on the agenda, this then also leads us to discuss the threats of safeguarding from radicalisation. Although this is reserved for chapter three, some light will be shed upon it here.

It is highly suggested within governmental reviews and publications (e.g. *Working together to safeguard children 2013*) that children are best raised by their parents, rather than by the state. However, ongoing concerns inform us that this may need to be reconsidered. Parents that advocate or impose extreme views upon their children with a view of encouraging them towards acts of violence or even towards support of terrorism have clearly abandoned their responsibilities to safeguard. This must be viewed by the state as clear contravention of parental responsibility, given the various publications and legislations discussed earlier. On this point, a publication released in the 'The Australian News' that discusses issues on national and world affairs, informs us that security experts

---

32   HM Government – Working together to safeguard children, 2013.

were concerned about parents radicalising their own children. This has been recognised as a serious problem not just in Australia but globally. On the same line of thinking, this would lead to tremors in the UK that would put considerable strain on the Children Act by reason of s17(1), which emphasises that, *'so far is consistent with that duty, to promote the upbringing of such children by 'their families', by providing a range and level of services appropriate to those children's needs'*[33] It is these and similar concerns that must be subjected to immediate, and not prolonged, inquiry or investigations. Whilst on this point, I must also bring to our attention that this would seem to challenge governmental publications that strongly suggest partnership working with parents is always in the interest of the child. Critically, given our opening chapter's that provides some evidence of a father who intends to indoctrinate his children with terrorism material, would prompt a drastic re-examination on the aforementioned governmental publications. In turn, this could lead to further reforms, policies and publications.

At this stage, a brief synopsis of our research certainly highlights the magnitude of the problem that faces us, and prompts us to consider the qualitative responses available at our disposable, chiefly 'early prevention'. In this orientation, the Prevent agenda was initially a problematic venture, labelled with criticism about its ability to deliver programmes of any credibility without being tempted to tamper with any information, because of its connection to government. This was hardly surprising, given there are strong views and to some extent evidence surrounding the authenticity of governmental programmes that have gained a reputation that they are more concerned about gathering intelligence and are geared towards spying, than they are about genuinely looking out for the interests of young people. Prime examples of the type mistrust and lack of confidence towards governments were seen during 2011. The UK riots, was an opportunity for young people to vent their grievances and anger against society. What had initially started out as a routine police check and investigation in London, had spiralled out of control. The death of a young black man angered a nation; this led to violent scenes all over the UK. Conflicting reports following these riots, suggested that the police were to be blamed for the shooting of unarmed black man and the governments were blamed for not having addressed the needs of disadvantaged and marginalised groups, especially in terms of youth unemployment and poverty. This had damaged any previous relationship the government had with young people and is still a problem that exists today. A swift response was required to quickly alleviate these apprehensions and anxieties, even more now within

---

33   The Children Act 1989, s(17).

this context of extremism. This is further discussed in chapter four. It would certainly not be over enthusiastic to suggest both safeguarding the welfare and the notion of significant harm have been taken even more seriously post 7/7 given the terrifying prospect that children could be used as 'human explosives or detonators' alarmed many, including the general public. Because of this, and in recognition of the grooming, recruitment and radicalisation of children and young people mobilised governments towards an offensive position; by this I simply mean, 'taking the bull by the horns'. Their contribution was a meaningful effort to respond. This also brought about the unity of specialist services into another territory.

Another area of improvement was seen with a police led project called Channel set up in 2006 by ACPO (Association of Chief Police Officers) their explicit purpose to provide support and towards offering specialist intervention for the more serious and high risk referrals that were expected to come through the doors. Channel was set to receive a range of high risk referrals from those, including local authorities, police, statutory partners, education, youth and social services. Channel was loaded with a wealth of information and those external agencies that were contemplating to engage in counter-terrorism work were expected to gain strength from within these realms. Correspondingly, a document entitled *Channel: protecting vulnerable people from being drawn into terrorism, a guide for local partnerships*[34] provided the platform in terms of raising awareness and providing the operational systems to share information. The document,-which explores the issues of identification,-explains in detail the ways in which a person can be drawn towards terrorism and become vulnerable to radicalisation. Its range of indicators consisted of the following referral criteria; *use of inappropriate languages, possession of violent extremist literature, behavioural changes, the expression of extremist views, advocating violent actions and means, association with known extremists and seeking to recruit others to an extremist ideology*[35]. Principally, these indicators were tasked with recognising distinct behaviour, signs and triggers that were similar to those displayed by children and young people engaged in problematic or violent behaviour. Some of these have been classified as anti-social, criminal and offending behaviour. This document was also advantageous in terms of raising awareness and for safeguarding the welfare of children and young people from these potential risks. It provided a criterion

34   Channel: protecting vulnerable people from being drawn into terrorism, a guide for local partnerships (October 2010).

35   Channel: protecting vulnerable people from being drawn into terrorism, a guide for local partnerships (October 2010).

that essentially comprised of the following: engagement with a group, cause or ideology, intent to cause 'harm', and capability to cause 'harm'. Its formal launch during 2006 saw a minimum of five referrals, astonishingly, this figure rose to approximately 748 during 2007/08. On par with this, there have been an estimated 44,000 young people that have attended 'preventing violent extremism' programmes across the UK since the since the terrorist attacks in 2005. These figures were expected to rise.

As we can clearly gather, this nexus of children and young people referred to programmes of extremism intervention has been far from scarce. These rationalities warranted many professionals to embrace this agenda more earnestly. Many professionals, in particular social workers, partly prepared by reason of their current role in relation to safeguarding children's and young people's welfare, sought to embrace the challenges this brought head on, a challenge they were initially unprepared for. Aspects pertaining to social workers' formal training and first-hand experience of conducting core assessment provided some of the fuel to arrive at this destination. This was further supplemented with extensive fieldwork practice with children and young people within various social environments. The use of conducting assessments was a driving force in many ways and in terms of development this has significance within preventing extremism and certainly gave scope for these skills to flourish within this agenda. In terms of assessment preferences, topping the list of nominations as the most highly decorated and accessible to a wide range of services would be the Common Assessment Framework, otherwise known as the CAF. However, prior to this venture, the need to educate professionals on terrorism agendas was necessary for a number or reasons. This would come with its own challenges, which is discussed further in chapter four.

CAF (Common Assessment Framework) initially introduced in 2005, became one of the most likely candidates, springing into action with a string of advantages to its assessment type. Unknown in this capacity before and with voluntary appeal, it was one of the stream that has brought about significant change. This was advantageous. Its resume has amassed a remarkable international cohort of registered nations, that recently in 2011, boasted 2,382 public sector organisations from 43 countries, registered as CAF users according to a CAF database. For many professionals, its pre-assessment and voluntary appeal was ideal for this internal environment, which attempted to minimise any complexities, without the headaches of any legal attachment, unlike many statutory court orders. By gaining the written consent of parents, this correspondence enabled professionals to penetrate families' dynamics and alert children's services to the potential risks or threats of possible extremism within these enclosed environments. Once established, the task of filtering potential referrals for specialist intervention would prove too complex for professionals alone to distinguish and required expert input. Once again, the expertise and collaboration with CTU (Counter-Terrorism Officers) or for less intensive and rigorous responses Prevent workers (see chapter five), were summoned to help facilitate this process – points that will be expounded later on. Initially, CAF strengthened prospects of identifying any early signs or risks through this medium and was the vehicle to transport this information across a wide range of sectors. In this sense, the potential of a network dynamic within child care sectors evolved. Moreover, Its practicality would provide the perfect 'social camouflage' that would minimise suspicions especially from sceptical families (as underpinning intentions to detect extremism or terrorism could not be made known for obvious reasons) given that many parents contested the notion that their children would even dare to entertain or engage in extremism with known local groups, let alone terrorism activity. Authorities such as Birmingham City Council have been instrumental in implementing such a process. This was not as straightforward as envisaged. This ran the risk of triggering aggressive confrontations at the expense of professionals' safety, and protecting staff during this process and in these environments was equally as paramount. Other concerns were seen with the repeated danger of this just becoming just another monitoring tool, which, according to Lord Laming, the CAF is *in danger, like other tools, of becoming process-focussed or, even worse, a barrier to services for children where access to services depends on a completed CAF form'* (Laming, 2009:42). A sharper focus is therefore required, especially at this early stage. Of course, the impending action for the more serious matters of safeguarding would become necessary. In child protection terms, these could be in the form of s47 inquiry for the more serious cases with subsequent child protection plans implemented as a precautionary measure. This invites other questions. It must be borne in mind, that the use of child protection as a means of legal action must also be validated. In this sense, the use of context and distinction are important when taking legal action. For example, *'reasonable cause to believe'* or *'reasonable cause to suspect'* could either hinder or accelerate this process and displace any possible early intervention to the detriment of the child or young person, which, as we have been repeatedly discussing, needs to be avoided.

In summarising, our analysis above has caused us to arrive at some conclusions. The events of July 7th 2005 have certainly suggested that *'safeguarding has some tangible and developing connections to extremism'* at least in particular reference to the potential and present dangers to child welfare, exploitation and harm. Moreover, the many catastrophic episodes of extremism and terrorism activities in the UK since 7/7 have become regular occurrences. To reiterate, the brutal killing of Drummer Lee Rigby in 2013, has awoken social workers, youth workers, social psychologists, teachers, community workers, criminologists and other like-minded professionals, to become more intricate, inquisitive and curious not just on topics or subjects exclusive to their professions, but more specifically, towards the risk and threats that violent extremism presents to children and young people. Yet, for many, especially social workers, it is still early days in coming to grips with agendas on preventing violent extremism, which is constantly evolving. We shall gather some insight from chapter two in relation to how wide and menacing this problem has become.

2: Current Risks and Threats

'We will continue to stop most [terrorist attacks] but we will not stop all of them'.

The former Director General of the Security Service,
Baroness Eliza Manningham-Buller 2006,

The periodic burst of terrorism activity has continued to escalate into the twentieth-first century. The number of casualties that are recorded as being direct result of a terrorist attack, has gradual gown, reaching into the hundreds and thousands, making this the loss of life in terms of any one violent action or event even more devastating. It is interesting to note that terrorism activity in the UK dates back over 100 years. This track record was oblivious to many before the terrifying events of 2005, which has thrived from a compilation of drivers and triggers. In fact, the use of the word terror has also been cited in religious manuscripts thousands of years earlier. Because of this and other factors, the threat of terrorism in the UK has rapidly evolved.

The use of the word 'terror' was first recorded during the 17th century. This was associated with the French revolution's 'reign of 'terror'. This 'reign of terror' in France, which killed approximately 40,000 people, was a drastic attempt to employ violence, including mass executions by guillotine, in order to intimidate the regime's enemies to compel obedience to the state. Its first recorded account in English was during 1798. However, I will extend and expound on this term from a theological perspective, and propose that the use of the word *'terror'* also has a theological heritage, dating back over 2,000 years. It was cited by one of the greatest apostles, Saint Paul (also known by his Jewish name Saul) during his missionary adventures during the periods of 33-67 AD. His persuasive use of the word *'terror'* is used primarily for evangelical and ecclesiastical purposes. Its proselytising emphasis has been mentioned only once in Saint Paul's second epistle to the Church located at Corinth, informing them that *'knowing therefore the 'terror' of the lord we persuade men'*[36]. Generally, it is used to describe the pending and current judgements of God as referred to in the Book of Revelation. In turn, this then leads us to examine its paralysing effect in the UK.

Prior to the threat of Islamic extremism to the UK, IRA terrorism remained the biggest threat. The IRA notoriously known for its ruthless

---

36   2nd Corinthians 5 v 1-11 The Holy Bible KJV (King James Version).

campaigns of terror (though not suicide bombings as such) had perpetrated Ireland-related bombings in the UK dating back as far as the 1880s. These were in drastic efforts to persuade British governments to grant home-rule to Ireland. This intensified and the list of casualties would grow, including children[37]. In one case, a bomb planted near a barracks in Salford in January 1881 killed a seven year old boy. London would also experience a catalogue of attacks during 1883-1885, which would include two underground trains, the House of Commons, the Tower of London and even the police headquarters at Scotland Yard. These actions led the Metropolitan Police to introduce the first police unit to combat terrorism in 1883, known as *Special Branch*. A more comprehensive account and history of these events are housed in the scholarly work of Dr Steve Hewitt's *The British War on Terror*. To date, the death toll from IRA-related bombings in the UK would remain the largest, with the highest recorded deaths from the Birmingham pub bombings in 1974, which are estimated at 21 killed and 182 injured. This would eventually be superseded in 2005 when 52 were killed and when the first ever recorded act of suicide bombing in the history of the UK terrorism took place. Since then the rise of terrorism and extremism activity in the UK has continued to grow.

Given the events of September the 11th 2001 terror attacks and the decision to 'go to war', the previous Labour Prime Minister (Tony Blair) had acknowledged that the Iraq War in 2003 had some 'blowbacks' which have clearly contributed to the rise of terrorism activity, not just in the UK but worldwide. A point that has repeatedly been cited by terrorism experts Peter Bergen and Paul Cuickshank, *'the Iraq war has generated a stunning sevenfold increase in the yearly rate of fatal jihadist attacks'* and that other sources indicated in 2005 that *'hundreds of terrorism suspects were under MI5 surveillance*[38] and again, according to a publication by the *Times* newspaper in 2005, '*10,000 people have attended extremism conferences'*.

Continuing on this notion, a press conference held on the 5th August 2005 just days after the July London bombings, Tony Blair had emphatically stressed that, *'let no one be in any doubt that the rules of the game had changed'*[39]. The Blair administration promised tougher measures to tackle this new threat. His newly formed *'12 point plan'* to fight terrorism was another string to his bow. The following year, the Prevent agenda would be summoned and subsequently

---

37   Dr Steve Hewitt 'The British War on Terror'.

38   Charles Clarke to Parliament 2005.

39   Tony Blair, Speech to TUC, 2005.

deployed to deliver counter-terrorism work within the UK. The current Prime Minister, David Cameron (given the pending election on 7th may 2015) has continued with the vision of Prevent, pledging to eradicate terrorism and extremism in the UK. The Prevent agenda has been amongst the government's most committed disciples in this sense; leading many towards mobilisation, given the threats of terrorism activity within the UK were expected to rise. Prevent depended on its ability to awaken services throughout the UK and to focus its efforts more widely, given its immense responsibility. On this point, Prevent sought to take matters further afield. What had yet to be thoroughly explored, however, and which is still (at the time of writing) largely scarce in academia and research was the task of safeguarding children and young people from the dangers of extremism and to what extent were these vulnerabilities open enough to create opportunities for extremists to exploit. These continue to keep security services on their feet.

The manifold threads in this chapter will largely focus on the risks to children and young people both in terms of their solicited recruitment and on the other hand, expounding upon the disturbing trend revolving around their voluntary participation. What is also evidenced before our very eyes are the testimonies of antiquity, which are housed particularly in religious extremist traditions that explain their longstanding practices to challenge democratic systems and governances, irrespective of their superiority. On this notion, there are clear implications, indications and strong connotations, that the action of religious extremists in particular, in recruiting British born individuals, is one that is idiosyncratic and that is pre-occupied to challenge the content of British values and to persuade its followers by offering an alternative and is one of considerable importance to our study. On this point, sociologist Bjoro has provided some insight to these dynamics. He explains and points out that a person (or groups for that matter) that possess the capability to 'change something' by 'influencing the sequences of something' has been as dominant and influential factor, not just with those in political arenas, but also among terrorists and those holding extremist views and therefore, cannot be underestimated, even if, in my view, they are children or young people.

In light of the aforementioned threats, security services have recognised the distinct trend of UK nationals becoming radicalised at home. What was yet to be discovered in this trend, however, was the sophisticated tactics used to groom, recruit and then radicalise them - an enigma which has continued to baffle many experts and professionals even today, let alone the social care professionals for which this book is intended. The sophistications and habitual practices of extremists have influenced a wide range of political and security measures. Since 2005, this has included financial contributions to counter-terrorism responses, resources and statistics. However, I must stress that the use of statistics in this sense, do not sufficiently or adequately explain how children and young people are radicalised but provide the evidence that threats from terrorists and extremists is certainly suggestive of its overall accomplishments. More conspicuously, the unprecedented rise of manpower within counter-terrorism agendas at all levels, clearly implies that this has been a costly rendition and suggests that such responses by security services alone is to some extent 'unmanageable and out of range'. Because of these limitations the dire urgency to incorporate a wider task force capable of covering a larger remit was consigned to governments to respond.

Even more disturbing, videos have been found in which young persons in the United Kingdom filmed themselves re-enacting beheadings. The youths were copying videos of beheadings that had been posted online by terrorist groups or their supporters.[40] Moreover, in 1998 there was a total of 12 active terrorist-related websites; by 2003 approximately 2,630; and by January 2009 a total of 6,940 active terrorist-related websites.[41] Because of this and other concerns, in 2013 David Cameron had set up the 'Extreme Task Force'. The aim being to identify any areas where current approaches were lacking and to agree practical steps that will fight all forms of extremism. Since coming to power, the coalition government has removed 18,000 on-line terrorist propaganda sites[42]. It is here that any doubt that extremism no longer exists within our society has evaporated from our minds; arguably it is on the increase, as we shall explore. Because of this technological advancement, which is an exclusive force in many ways, the use of technology to recruit individuals has not made matters easier and is widely incorporated in terrorism recruitment, a point that has been repeatedly cited by a terrorism expert, Bruce Hoffman from Georgetown University, USA. According to Bruce Hoffman, *virtually every terrorist group in the world today has its own Internet website and, in many instances, multiple sites in different languages with different messages tailored to specific audiences.* The radicalisation of individuals through these portals

---

40   7 P.W. Singer, The New Children of Terror, The Making of a Terrorist: Recruitment, Training and Root Causes, vol. 1, ed. James J.F. Frost, (Praeger, November 2005), 105-119.

41   13 Dr. Gabriel Weimann, The Internet as a Terrorist Tool to Recruit Youth (presentation given at the Youth Recruitment & Radicalisation Roundtable, Arlington, Virginia, March 19, 2009).

42   HM Tackling extremism - the UK report from the Prime Minister's task force on tackling radicalisation and extremism.

has been demonstrated with many cases ranging from the July 7th bombers to 'lone wolf crusaders' such as Nicky Riley.

SECURITY SERVICES' CONCERNS

In 2007, the previous head of MI5 Jonathan Evans, had expressed his immediate concerns related to the UK. He categorically stated that, *'extremists were methodically and intentionally targeting young people and children in the UK, and that groups like Al-Qaeda were recruiting children as young as 15 years old to wage a deliberate campaign of terror in Britain'*. Moreover importantly, in his first memorable speech whilst taking office, Mr Evans warned that extremists were *'radicalising, indoctrinating and grooming young, vulnerable people to carry out acts of terrorism,'* and that urgent action was required on the part of the UK government *'to protect its children from exploitation by violent extremists'*. The continued threat had the similar potential for another July 7th which, as we are now fully aware off, left several hundred injured. Ongoing reports have indicated that police are foiling a terrorism plot as big as the 7th July attacks every year, according to one senior officer. Deputy Assistant Commissioner Stuart Osborne added that the threats against the UK were constantly changing and Mr Osborne, senior national coordinator for counter-terrorism, said, *'Islamic extremists were planning in smaller groups to avoid detection'*. It was hardly surprising that MI5 would see an unprecedented growth in their caseloads.

The former director of CIA (Central Intelligence Agency) Michael Hayden, on the subject of Al-Qaeda, echoed a similar point to that of MI5, that such groups were actively seeking youths from western countries because of their familiarity with the language, culture and appearance and would therefore, as he states, *'not illicit any notice whatsoever, from you if they were standing next to you in the airport'*. With this in mind it is hardly surprising that Al-Qaeda have referred to children in the past as the, *'new generation of Mujahidin'*. Former head of MI5, Baroness Eliza Manningham-Buller, had also expressed her views saying that *'she was not surprised that the 7/7 suicide bombers in London were British'*. When questioned during the Chilcot inquiry into the UK's role into Iraq, she replied, *'Our involvement in Iraq radicalised, for want of a better word, a whole generation of young people - not a whole generation, a few among a generation-who saw our involvement in Iraq and Afghanistan as being an attack upon Islam'*[43]. We must remind ourselves that extremists and terrorists have continued to develop their operations from

---

43   The Chilcot Inquiry.

within the UK. These efforts will seek to foster and radicalise a whole new generation on British soil and of British origin, fitting perfectly well with their global idea and objective.

Moreover, post 7/7 it was estimated that around 2,000 individuals have attended training camps abroad and returned to the UK with possibilities of coordinating terrorist attacks. The ring leader of the July 7th 2005 Bombings, Siddique Khan, had also engaged in such activities abroad before killing himself in July. Evidence to the CLG (Communities Local Government) select committee from ACPO (Association Chief Police Officers) highlighted the fact that one of the July 7th bombers, Hasib Hussain, had drawn graffiti in support of Bin Laden and 9/11 attacks on his exercise books whilst at high school in Leeds. Similarly, Jermaine Lindsey, one of the July 7th bombers, attempted to access radical Islamist websites whilst at high school in Huddersfield. Furthermore, past reports warned that at least three separate Al-Qaeda related operations had involved people who became involved in extremism while they were at school, including the July 7th and Transatlantic Airways plots. According to the New York City Police Department, since 9/11 jihadists comprising 70 nationalities have been captured in about 100 countries around the world. The threat is global and it is on our doorsteps. A BBC news interview televised on the 17th October 2014, revealed that Scotland Yard have responded to at least *'100 terror threats a week'*. As a result of Islamist terrorism, the rise of far-right extremism has also gained ground, in reputation as well as casualties. The alarming attendance of young people at far-right demonstrations in the UK cannot be overlooked as could not the tragic killing in Europe of 73 young people who were attending a political activists' camp in Oslo, Norway in 2011, by Anders Breivik a far-right Christian extremist. These investigations would lead back to the UK.

The police were investigating links between Anders Breivik and the far-right within the UK, after Prime Minister David Cameron had called for checks. At a meeting of the National Security Council the Prime Minister requested the checks following revelations that Anders Breivik may have met with British fascists. In a 'manifesto' the gunman published online shortly before the attacks, he mentioned far-right groups in the UK, including the EDL (English Defence league) and detailed that immigrants were undermining Norway's traditional Christian values, identifying himself as a *'Christian Crusader'*. The allegations concerning the XRW in UK were denied by the EDL who stressed in a statement that, *'Breivik talks about the EDL in a negative light because of our anti-extremist stance'*. The Prime Minister's official spokesman said, '*we should ensure we have adequate scrutiny of the behaviour of extremist individuals and groups*'. We cannot deny, though groups such as the EDL may not have engaged in any act of full-blown terrorism (as far as we know) but the potential for violent behaviour is highly decorated within their 'extreme views' which are cognitively rehearsed, especially in terms of '*inciting racial and religious hatred*' - points often referred to by Dr Matthew Goodwin, a leading expert on the far right. The EDL, on the point of incitement and lacking in racial understanding, must be reminded that the term 'race' is meaningless in scientific terms, in that the concept is a social and political construct. Undoubtedly then, the behaviour of these groups has further threatened the harmonisation of communities and the social integration of others. This would create the ideal atmosphere allowing segregation to flourish, which in turn, could also drive some towards other forms of extremism and at worst, towards becoming radicalised. Indeed, it is precisely because of groups like these that there is an underpinning element that may provide, according to one researcher, '*pathway to extremism by genuinely defending rights in favour of democratic society*'. Of course, this is disturbing, given that Anders Breivik's 'Hitler-style salutes' have been applauded by some who have stressed he is defending 'Christian values'. In another report we are informed that a man from the West-Midlands sought petitions for Breivik's release and left a message on Facebook stating that, '*he is truly inspirational*'. This raises serious concerns for the UK.

Continuing on the point of security concerns, America would make similar appeals. Speaking to the United Nations, President Barack Obama made an urgent appeal to Muslim youth to reject the 'cancer of violent extremism' infecting the Muslim world. Claiming the U.S. will 'dismantle' the 'network of death' that is the Islamic State, Obama said it's clear the world is determined to root out the 'cancer of violent extremism;' noting: '*The only language understood by killers like this is the language of force. So the United States of America will work with a broad coalition to dismantle this network of death.*' Obama spoke at length directly to the Muslim world and, in particular, Muslim youth: '*Those who have joined ISIL should leave the battlefield while they can. Those who continue to fight for a hateful cause will find they are increasingly alone. ... The future belongs to those who build – not those who destroy.*'[44] I must point out, that the terrorist attacks of September 11th 2001 certainly gave rise to a greater impetus on the fight against terrorism, especially in countries such as America. For example, crime fighting agencies such as

---

44   President Barack Obama, speech to United Nations 2014.

the FBI (Federal Bureau of Investigation) have gradually shifted their main priority since 9/11 from crime to terrorism. This also saw specialist security departments installed, for example, the Department for Homeland Security, unheard of until after the terrorist attacks on 9/11. President Obama has continued to summarise the global threat of extremism. At a press conference held by President Obama, which was attended by David Cameron during his visit to America in January 2015, President Obama referred to radicalisation as 'a poisonous ideology'. From these points its continue to uphold the legitimacy of this global threat. Almost simultaneously, the recent meeting of the World Economic Forum held in France during January 2015, attended by US Secretary Kerry, had referred to the wider problems and misconceptions of narrowing extremism. He stressed 'it's an *'error' to refer to violent extremism as Islamist alone'*, whilst on the other hand, British Foreign Secretary Phillip Hammond stood next to Kerry and urged the defeat what he called the *'scourge of violent Islamist extremism'* referring to the attacks in Australia in December 2014 and in France 2015.

International crime fighting agencies such as Interpol, have provided a similar position pertaining to the threats of extremism involving young people. They stressed that the radicalisation of youth was a serious issue, emphasising that, *'beyond the obvious threat it poses to global safety and security, moreover, 'Preventing radicalisation' is a particularly complex challenge for law enforcement because many of the behaviours associated with it are not in and of themselves criminal'*[45]. In not underestimating the potential of young people, the mastermind behind the Bali, Indonesia, bombings in 2002 was by all accounts executed by a star pupil with a bright future and let's not forget that in 2008, a young man of Somali descent, became, authorities believe, the first American citizen to carry out a suicide bombing. He and others like him escaped that country's instability as refugees, only to return from the United States as extremists. Estimates believe that there is a gradual decline in extremism and terrorism age. In France, in 1998, the average age of individuals arrested on terrorism-related charges was 32 years old. By 2005 that figure had dropped to 21 years. The recruiters are smart. They target young, vulnerable individuals by offering what parents often view as a safer alternative to gangs and 'Transform living rooms into radical madrassas.' Furthermore, Interpol, searching for two girls form Austria, one aged 16 years old and the other 15 years old from Bosnian refugee families, admitted to concerns over their links to terrorism.

---

45   www.interpol.int

The impact of the media on the threat of extremism cannot be under-estimated. A Sky News report in February 2015, informed us that police were assessing Al Shabaab threats to the US and the UK. According to the report, Islamist militants had released a video, in which they appeared to call for terrorist attacks on some of the busiest shopping areas in the US and the UK. The video had specifically mentioned Oxford Street and Shepherds Bush in London. The US authorities have taken these threats seriously, given that it was Somali based militants that had claimed responsibility for the 2013 attack on an upmarket shopping mall in Kenya, which left 67 dead. Jen Johnson, the secretary chief of Homeland Security in the US said, '[A]nytime a terrorist organisation calls for an attack in a specific place, we've got to take that seriously.'

A Growing Trend

The last few years have proven to provide greater challenges to security services within the UK. Current trends of extremism recruitment within the UK have raised further concerns for national security as an estimated 500 Britons over the past three years have gone to Syria to fight, potentially making this country, as far as MI5 are concerned, *presenting a greater threat of radical-isation than even Iraq*[46]. An assessment by MI5 spells out how alluring Syria has become to UK jihadists, stating, *'The nature of the conflict in Syria and the emergence of Al-Nusra Front, which has declared its allegiance to Al-Qaeda leader Ayman al-Zawahiri, is leading to the country becoming an increasingly significant potential source of future threats to the UK and UK interests overseas'*[47]. These concerns were apparently confirmed to the Telegraph by an unnamed Whitehall contact. Furthermore, *'The threat to the UK comes from a range of countries and groups but Syria is perhaps the biggest challenge right now'* they explained. The Home office annual review likewise states that the country has been identified as *'the most significant development in global terrorism'*.

The conflicts in Syria have certainly created opportunities. Unlike terrorism hotbeds such as Afghanistan and Pakistan, Syria is much closer to Europe, making this an ideal destination to go and come back. One problem associated with identification and profiling, is that many returning jihadists from such countries do not fit the psychological profile of conventional terror-ists. The first British national in Syria, Abdul Waheed Majeed has become known as the first suicide attacker, who remained largely anonymous prior

---

46   MI5 cited.

47   MI5 cited.

to his departure to Syria. He was believed to have driven an explosive-laden truck into a jail in Aleppo during early May 2014, joining some 20 British Citizens to have died fighting in Syria. Problems faced by security services, as expressed by political commentator Mohammed Ansar on Russia Today, is that using Majeed's case, '*he does not fit the profile of a young British Jihadi who has gone to Syria to fight' adding* also that '*fighters from Britain have been calling others to come and join them*'[48]. He also concludes by saying that, '*studying the British jihadist motives will enable us to better understand how to deal with this rising problem'.* It also emerged in 2014, two 16 year old star college pupils from Chorlton, Manchester, had abandoned their homes to fly to a rapidly expanding warzone.

Dr Liam Fox, the former Defence Secretary, had previously warned that security forces must 'redouble' efforts to stop British-born jihadists returning home to kill citizens in the UK. In an article for the *Daily Telegraph* website, he said: '*When young jihadists develop the habit for hating it can be hard to break. Our security forces know that many do not lack the will to kill us, merely the capability. We will have to redouble our efforts to ensure that remains the case.*'[49] He continues to stress that there would be 'catastrophic' security consequences if extremism is not defeated, and urged the government to send British military assets to the region to assist any American-led attacks on ISIS, saying the UK '*should not rule out acting where we could provide specific help*' . It is also heart-breaking to know that another Britain would make international headlines in relation to terrorism. 'Jihadi John' which he would eventually become known as, had become the practical arms and feet of the violent extremist group ISIS. By beheading western hostages on behalf of this dangerous group, he has gained an international reputation that has sent fear all over the world. It was alleged that he was responsible for the beheading of US journalist James Foley in August 2014 and was known to be involved in other massacres in the name of Islam. His true identity which was often concealed through his attire and balaclava baffled many that were intrigued to know his true identity. Eventually, his true identity would be revealed by intelligence and security services such as the FBI and MI5. A BBC report disclosed in February 2015 revealed that this Kuwait-British born man was from west London and had moved to the UK in 1994. It was understood that he was aged about 27. We ask ourselves, how many more individuals with the same potential to terrorise innocent civilians are living within the UK?

---

48   Russia Today news.
49   Liam Fox, Daily Telegraph Website, 2014.

The metropolitan police assistant commissioner and counter-terrorism officer, Miss Cressida Dick, made her comments in an address to the Royal United Services Institute think-tank in 2014. She said, *'there is less 'alertness' among British Muslims about extremism compared with those in other countries'*. But she said *'violent images from Syria and Iraq were forcing them to confront the problem'*. Police were using the conflicts to try to convince families and friends to turn in loved ones if they suspected them of extremist activities. She said, *'In the UK we want to depend more on families, schools, friends, health professionals, employers, observing changes in such and having the confidence to come forward. We do have frequent examples of this, but also many examples of warning signs being missed, ignored or not being brought to the attention of the authorities'*. Another senior police official has backed Miss Dick's remarks. Sir Peter Fahy, the Chief Constable of Greater Manchester, said a lot of extremists were radicalised 'in their own community'.[50] He continued to stress that the 'police needed the whole of this community to counter this threat'.

Other terrorism experts suggest that this could be spiralling out of control. Richard Barrett, a former head of counter-terrorism at MI6, estimated that *'possibly up to 300 people have come back to the UK'* already, and warned that intelligence services faced an 'impossible' task in trying to track them. He told the *Independent on Sunday*, *'If you imagine what it would cost to really look at 300 people in depth, clearly it would be completely impossible to do that, probably impossible even at a third of that number'*[51] and that *'police and intelligence resources were stretched in terms of numbers and knowing where the returning jihadists are.'* Mr. Barrett has co-authored a report, which concludes that more than 12,000 foreign fighters have gone to Syria since the war began, and that it is *'likely to be an incubator for a new generation of terrorists'*. As an incubator, the UK could have the right climate, conditions and capacity to foster. Reports continued. The *Mail On-line* published on the 12th September 2014, *'British children under ten are being turned into 'junior Jihadists'* as extremists bombed them with dangerous propaganda. London Deputy Manager, Stephen Green Haigh responsible for the policing and crime for London said, due to the events of ISIS, said *'some of them are very young, it's pretty horrendous when you hear some of these children are being radicalised, the threat of radicalisation of young people is real and this is a problem that is going to be with us not just now or after*

50 http://www.dailymail.co.uk/news/article-2666460/UK-Muslims-complacent-threat-home-grown-jihadists-warns-counter-terrorism-officer-Cressida-Dick.html#ixzz3YJzaW0k3

51 The Independent 2014.

for a couple of years, but for the next generation[52]. This has led to various arrest.

Reports during early 2015, stated that anti-terror police from Great Manchester had arrested a boy and a girl aged 15 and 16 from Mossley, Tameside. The teens were held under suspicion of terror offences to do with the *'commissioning, preparation and inciting acts of terrorism'*. Investigating, Chief Superintendent Caroline Ball said, *'I know news of an arrest made under terrorism legislation in the community will cause a certain amount of anxiety and people will understandably have questions'* she continues, *'this investigation is as a result from law enforcement agencies so it's prudent we act on that information'*. Other reports have also emerged that some girls had planned to leave the UK to join ISIS. One of the girls, a so-termed 'terror brides for ISIS', had been in contact with known extremists, who left their Glasgow home during 2013 after becoming radicalised. Moreover, during March 2015 another 19 year old and two 17 year old school boys were arrested in the UK attempting to fly to the Syrian warzone. In another BBC news report aired on 19th April 2015, we were informed that police were investigating an entire family suspected of travelling to Syria. Mr Asif Malik, his wife and children aged 7, 4, 2 and 1 years old who were attending Claycotts Primary school in Slough - left the UK suddenly. It was feared they were on their way to Syria. Because of these and other concerns, security chiefs are increasingly desperate to get into often closed communities and understand what is attracting our young people to such a barbaric organisation. Another young man had been arrested by the police under terrorism legislation, when it was revealed that he had intentions to replicate Lee Rigby's murder. His previous association with the known extremist group Al-Muhajiroun was a contributory factor which the police said played a significant role in his radicalisation. He had also posted on his face book page that he was 'willing to die in the cause of Allah'. Brusthom Ziamani, aged 19 from Camberwell, South London, was arrested in August 2014. He was found with a knife and hammer in his possession. When questioned he said that he was inspired by those that had killed Drummer Lee Rigby in the spring of May 2013. It was later established that he had researched cadet bases looking for possible victims. Brusthom had heralded one of Lee Rigby's killers as a 'legend'. His arrest was a joint effort by the police and MI5. After Brusthom sentencing, Deb Walsh, deputy head of counter-terrorism at the Crown Prosecution Service said, '[*T]his case highlights how violent and extreme views on a page can become credible threats to the lives and safety of British citizens'.*

---

52   Source known.

Statistics have provided some insight of how serious the problem of extremism is becoming. For example, of the 127 convictions for terrorism-related offences associated with Al Qaeda, 11 have been committed by people in the age range of 15-19[53]. Information released under the Freedom of Information Act suggests that increasing numbers of children and young people have been referred to government project such as channel for intervention because of extremism concerns. For example, for those aged 11 years, 153 were referred; for those aged between 12-15, 690 were referred; and for those aged 16-17, 554 were referred from the periods between 2007 to January 2014. In another case, a teenage schoolboy in East Lancashire was referred to the Channel project for regularly drawing bombs and guns. Again, a three year old was involved because an entire family was referred. Schools are referring to the police record numbers of pupils identified as being at risk of radicalisation. Sir Peter Fahy, the Chief Constable of Manchester police who leads on extremism for ACPO (Association of Chief Police Officers), told the *Guardian* that schools were now the greatest source of concern for the police, followed by local authorities, the NHS and then higher education.

EDUCATIONAL CONCERNS

There is an estimated 8 million children attending various schools within the UK. The sheer numbers of children and young people attending education in the UK is growing and the need to safeguard them is equally as demanding. The Education Act 2002 (s) 175[54] introduced a new statutory duty on local education authorities, maintained and independent schools and further education institutions to ensure that their responsibilities are carried out with a view to safeguarding and promoting the welfare of children and young people. Because of this greater scrutiny of independent and faith schools were brought into serious question over alleged matters of extremism. More pointedly, problems have arisen, particularly in respect to faith schools' teaching material, some of which have been linked to extremism influence. With very little sympathy to extremism of any sort, the Prevent agenda has quite unreservedly voiced that *'the government is clear that there is no place for extremists in any school'*[55]. Because of this, the 'Preventing Extremism Unit' was established within the DfE (Department for Education) their aim to *'minimise the risk that unsuitable providers can set*

53 HM Prevent strategy, 2011.

54 Education Act 2002.

55 Prevent agenda 2011 s 10.48 (Objective three).

up *Free Schools'*. This venture warranted the expertise from counter-terrorism unit. Ofsted, having already acquired a prominence in the Prevent review, in reference to regulation, it was emphasised that *'working with DfE, Ofsted will ensure that inspectors have the necessary knowledge and expertise to determine whether extremist and intolerant beliefs are being promoted in school and then to take appropriate action*.'[56] A point well-rehearsed by NAHT General Secretary, Russell Hobby, who said, *'The way we educate our young people shapes the society we will live in. British schools have long been dedicated to encouraging students to think for themselves and to think about others, a blend of critical thinking and empathy that is the best inoculation against radicalism and extremism.'* The strategy also adds that the new set of standards for teachers, currently the subject of an independent review and work within the *DfE 'should better enable schools to take action against staff who demonstrate unacceptable views.'* The new set of standards will *'clarify obligations regarding extremism'*. The shadow business secretary, Chuka Umunna, said, *'more could be done in schools to give children an understanding about world affairs and to inform them about why things are happening'.* There are also wider implications regarding the lack of policies, especially within educational establishments which in turn can affect internal infrastructures and processes. This requires immediate action.

Under increased pressure, questions were raised by MPs surrounding the 'Trojan Horse Plot' at Parkview School, Small Heath, Birmingham, to take over, replacing the curriculum with an alternative in the form of disturbing 'hard-core Islamic material'. The presence of counter-terrorism officers at the school certainly threw suspicions over other educational establishments. This opened the door to a range of views, arguments and also community tensions. Imran Awan, senior lecturer in criminology at BCU (Birmingham City University) waded into the row, stressing that the repercussion of making rash judgements can throw suspicions on communities without considering the damaging effects these may have. These points need to be taken into account. In response to the current plot, Awan states, *'Trojan horse extremism myths are damaging community cohesion in Birmingham'*. He continues, *'to me the most significant outcome is loss of community cohesion and diversity, which was one of Birmingham's key strength'*. Government was in a difficult position, in response to these particular extremism concerns, and could not risk alienating the very communities which it had sought to integrate in Britain – efforts which could so easily have been sabotaged. Downing Street would have to exercise discreet responses. Given David Cameron's reputation was again at stake and, with the forthcoming elections on the horizon, could have proven counter-intuitive. His response was clear and in the most challenging tone;

'Protecting our children is one of the first duties of government and that is why the issue of alleged Islamist extremism in Birmingham schools demands a robust response. The Education Secretary will now ask Sir Michael Wilshaw to look into allowing any school to be inspected at no notice, stopping schools having the opportunity to cover up activities which have no place in our society'.

Following in the footsteps of David Cameron, the former Education Secretary Michael Gove stressed;

We have to ensure children are safe in our schools. Evidence uncovered in Birmingham clearly indicates that schools have used the notice they have been given of inspections to evade proper scrutiny. Sir Michael Wilshaw will now examine the practicalities of moving to a position where all schools know they may face an unannounced inspection...Our children need to be protected in schools, kept safe from the dangers of extremism and guaranteed a broad and balanced curriculum. This change will help provide parents with the reassurance they need.

In the House of Commons, Edward Timpson, answering questions from MPs about the Trojan Horse allegations of hard-line Muslim infiltration of classrooms in Birmingham, said, *'the government's Prevent strategy to identify and eradicate extremism had to be a priority for all schools'*. He continues, *'schools can help protect children from extremist and violent views in the same ways that they help to safeguard children from drugs, gang violence or alcohol abuse'*[57]. The previous Education Secretary Michael Gove had written to all schools and colleges in England urging them to watch out for signs of extremism in the wake of the so-called Trojan Horse plot. In a letter to head teachers, the Education Secretary said schools and colleges must be aware of any type of child abuse. He said this included cyber-bullying, sexual exploitation and female genital mutilation. The Department of Education advice included links to existing guidance from a variety of organisations. The information said those at risk might possess 'material or symbols associated with an extremist cause' (e.g. the swastika for far right groups). It added they *'spend increasing time in the company of other suspected extremists'* or *'attempt to recruit others to their cause'.*

Continuing to discuss this matter, in light of the Trojan Horse plot and schooling, serious questions have been brought to the forefront, pertaining

---

57 House of Commons, question session, 2014.

to the exclusive setting up of independent schools, vetting of their staff and safeguarding. Mohammed Shahid, a headmaster whose far-fetched views have been linked to known extremists, raised serious questions on vetting procedures. Moreover, the use of hard-line teaching to indoctrinate children within his faith school, raises further questions on how tight procedures and vetting processes were for those intending to register independent schools. The Department for Education has said it was 'urgently' looking into Shahid's case which, many have stressed, has exposed the lack of checks on potentially dangerous individuals who can set up schools in the UK. Lord Carlyle, the Government's former adviser on counter-terrorism legislation, said, '*It is a matter of real concern that somebody should be able to slip through the net and run a school where there has been substantial concern about his activities in the past. People who have been involved in terrorist activity anywhere in the world should not be allowed to run schools, unless there is the clearest evidence they have rejected the views that made them turn towards terrorism*'. Keith Vaz, chairman of the Home Affairs Committee which is investigating terrorism, including extremism in schools, said, '*It's extremely worrying a person with such a history, which should be of concern to the relevant authorities, should be in such a position. The DfE needs to look into this urgently*[58]. An article published in the *Daily Telegraph* in November 2014 has raised similar concerns. The Sir John Cass Foundation and Red Coat Church of England schools in Tower Hamlets, London, were under intense pressure from Ofsted regulators who have stated that the '*schools failed to safeguard pupils from extremism.*' These actions came to light when the school failed to safeguard pupils from radicalisation when they had set up a YouTube channel which was not monitored according to one report. Previous concerns of extremism in schools were ignored. The *Birmingham Mail* reported that Tim Boyes, head of Queens Bridge School in Moseley, had warned the government that some Birmingham pupils were showing signs of extremism four years before city schools were linked to the Trojan horse controversy and has highlighted schools which had allegedly suffered '*interference*', but that his concerns were seemingly never acted upon. Mr Boyes is reported as having given '*a powerful presentation to Lord Hill, then a schools minister in Education Secretary Michael Gove's department.*' This then, leads us to explore some of the most discussed issues of 'grooming, 'recruitment' and 'radicalisation' in more detail.

---

58   Keith Vaz, Home Affairs Select Committee.

3: Children, Young People and Radicalisation – Understanding Theories and Concepts

'When young men born and bred in this country are radicalised...we have to ask some tough questions...it is as if for some young people there is a conveyer belt to radicalisation...we need to dismantle this process at every stage. In schools, colleges, universities, on the internet, in our prisons – wherever it is taking place.'

Prime Minister, David Cameron, 3rd June 2013.

There are several caveats that are of considerable importance and that are crucial towards understanding the cause of extremism and terrorism. Because of the complicated nature of terrorism, it requires some treatment to ensure we grasp a clear understanding. Needless to say comprehending essential terms such as terrorism and radicalisation are somewhat traumatising. Hence, distinctions and consolidations are necessary. Further insight in this particular chapter, will grant us access to some of the views and definitions that are in circulation from a wide range of standpoints. This will also open the reader's mind to the inter-connectedness of terrorism to religion, and vice-versa. This will enable tighter safeguarding measures to be considered. I will saturate the reader's mind with some of the preferred definitions which are widely shared, that, in my view, are applicable for professionals working with children and young people. The definitions that I will refer to have generally been accepted as comprising the necessary components and are proportionate in defining the processes associated with radicalisation. Some of these views are widely embedded in training, academia, publications and research. It has also become noticeable that the uses of these terms have also contributed to many misunderstandings, it is within this chapter that these need to be reflected on to minimise these misunderstandings.

Before we start I would like to point out that, in briefly sharing one of my experiences, whilst delivering a lecture on counter-terrorism, I had to referee a heated discussion between students, this revolving around who was the real terrorist, given the argument that arose 'one man's terrorist is another man's freedom fighter'. These oppositions were situated in two camps, western government and Muslims defending their country. Other interesting views arose pertaining to the theories surrounding the attacks of September 11th 2001 and July 7th 2005 Bombings with particular emphasis on the Bush and Blair administrations. The reason for saying that, no matter where you are in the world, your views, your concepts or what you believe, it is abundantly clear, that terrorism is a subject that has attracted a 'worldwide audience' with a 'worldwide contribution'. With that said, we shall discuss these points further.

DEFINITIONS OF RADICALISATION AND TERRORISM

Far from embracing the nuances of terrorism, one of the many predicaments currently faced by social work and other professionals is primarily concerned with comprehending the terms associated with this new agenda - the numerous suggestions, exhortations and views used throughout have added to this predicament. In fact, the many contentions associated with this agenda have dominated many confrontations worldwide. The most obvious are defining terrorism, and defining who is a terrorist. This is an ideal starting point.

Terrorism is a fiercely contested concept. It is also a global phenomenon which is easy to recognise but difficult to define. It has been repeatedly voiced that terrorism has over 100 definitions, which, in terms of scope cannot be covered here in detail. While some of the definitions may be rejected, they cannot be totally abandoned, given the views offered have tenable relevance for our study. I have chosen a couple to illustrate this point. A favourable one, as discussed in our introduction, is seen with Martha Crenshaw's definition. Crenshaw, from the University of Maryland and since 2005, current lead for National Consortium for the Study of Terrorism and Responses to Terrorism, describes terrorism as, *'a particular style of political violence, including attacks on a small number of victims in order to influence a wider audience'.* In the same vein, I would extend on the latter point, stressing, *'in order to influence children and young people to the glamour of violent extremism'.* Alex P Schmid, a Dutch scholar on terrorism and Director of the Centre for the Study of Terrorism and Political Violence, St Andrews University, Scotland, gives a lengthy definition, *'Terrorism is an anxiety-inspiring method of repeated violent action, employed by (semi-) clandestine individual, group or state actors, for idiosyncratic, criminal or political reasons, whereby - in contrast to assassination - the direct targets of violence are not the main targets. The immediate human victims of violence are generally chosen randomly (targets of opportunity) or selectively (representative or symbolic targets) from a target population, and serve as message generators.*

Threat- and violence-based communication processes between terrorist (organisation), (imperilled) victims, and main targets are used to manipulate the main target (audience(s)), turning it into a target of terror, a target of demands, or a target of attention, depending on whether intimidation, coercion, or propaganda is primarily sought.' For the purpose of our study these are worth storing. I must also inform the readers before we proceed, that an *'ideology often refers to a belief system often political or religious, typically hallmarked by extremism and terrorism.'* On another note ,the MI5 Behavioural Science Unit has also stressed that, *'there is no typical pathway to extremism';* with this in mind, we will proceed.

Taking these illustrious views into consideration, these inform us of some of the fundamental components that describe the characteristics of terrorism. As you begin to read, you will gather that this implies the collective and the repeated use of 'violence' or the 'threat of the use of violence' as an major component and objective to its advancement. Legal definitions have also referred to the use of violence as integral to terrorism advancement. One of its earliest forms recorded in the UK was showcased in the following, *'section 2(2) of the Reinsurance (acts of terrorism) Act 1993, which defines terrorism as, 'acts of person, action on behalf, or in connection with, any organisation which carries out activities directed towards the overthrowing or influencing by force or violence of Her Majesty's government in the United Kingdom, or any other government, de jure or de facto'.* The current definition on terrorism, has been somewhat extended and built on by these and other international fears. With this in mind, the Terrorism Act 2000 defines terrorism as;

The means the use or threat of action where the use of threat designed to influence the government or to intimidate the public or a section of the public, and (c) the use of threat is made for the purpose of advancing a political, religious or ideological cause, and Action falls within the subsection if it; (a) involves serious violence against a person, (b) involves damage to property, (c) endangers a person's life, other than that of the person committing the action, (d) creates serious risk to the health or safety of the public or a section of the public, (e) is designed seriously to interfere with or seriously disrupt an electronic system[59].

We are left with very little choice but to accept the legal definition for a variety of reasons, for example, given that the notion of violence is a prolific driver in terrorism's advancement assures us that enforcement is necessary to prevent terrorists from flourishing and to send warning signals to those who have intentions to engage in such acts. However, after saying that, many have

---

59   Terrorism Act 2000.

contested and protested against legal definitions which seem to criminalise those with legitimate views even if they are in contradistinction to British values. In spite of the many contentions, views or opinion, the legal definition would prevail. One of the primary reasons is the explicit use of words such as 'threat' and 'violence' and given the prospect that terrorists promise to advance their cause through the 'use of violence' was a critical factor in this conclusion as was the risk presented to the wider public and the state. We have also been reminded of existing criminal laws that inform us that any behaviour which incorporates the use of physical violence without the presence of any political or ideological drivers or motivation has been subject to sanctions and prosecutions. This has been long-standing with crimes such as *wounding with intent*[60] and *grievous bodily harm*[61]. It is becoming more clearer that some of these violent behaviours have crossed-over into extremism environments, but the severity of these are not sufficient enough to be deemed a threat to national security or for those engaged in these acts to have any intention of dethroning governments, unlike those with terrorist intent. In this distinction, it is well established that unlike crime, terrorism is politically motivated.

A range of these criminal behaviours can be found in the following enactments; Offence against the Person Act 1861 (s18-20) Criminal Law Act 1977, the Criminal Justice Act 1994, the Protection from Harassment Act 1997, the Police Act 1997, the Crime and Disorder Act 1998 (s28-32, s29), the Anti-social Behaviour Act 2003, the Criminal Justice Act 2003 and the Serious Organised Crime and Police Act 2005. On this point, we must also be aware that these were designed to control public behaviour. Given these and the aforementioned definitions and the notion of the use violence as a benchmark, both the past and current government independent reviewers of UK terrorism legislation (Lord Carlyle 2001-2011 and David Anderson QC 2011 - present) have reiterated on numerous occasions that *'terrorism is a crime'.* In finalising this point, the conditional element that must be prevalent amongst all extreme groups and that must be an 'active agent' before we can expound or entertain any argument that suggests that any form of radicalisation will lead to an act of terrorism, is again the obvious use of 'violence'. It is here that we will consume definitions of radicalisation that incorporate and ultimately lead to violence.

The Dutch intelligence service AVID, states that radicalisation is, *'the active pursuit of support to far-reaching changes in society which may constitute a danger to (the continued existence of the democratic legal order (aim) which*

---

60   Offence Against the Person Act 1861 s18.

61   Ibid s 18 and 20.

may involve the use of violence of undemocratic methods (means) that may harm the functioning of the democratic legal order (effect), supplemented by person's (growing) willingness to pursue and/or support changes himself (in an undemocratic way or otherwise) or his encouraging others to do. AVID 2004. Pp. 13-14[62]) or phrased a bit shorter, as it is done by the Danish intelligence services;

'Radicalisation can be described as a process, by which a person to an increasing extent accepts the use of undemocratic or violent means including terrorism, in an attempt to reach a specific political/ideological objective'. PET (pg1)

One definition presented by Royal Canadian Mounted Police (RCMP) described the process by which, *'individuals are introduced to an overtly ideological message and belief system that encourages movement from moderate, mainstream beliefs towards extreme views'*. EU policy makers have formed some definitions. A particular one used by the European commission, is a frequently applied definition of violent radicalisation accordingly, *'The phenomenon of people embracing opinions, views and ideas which could lead to acts of terrorism' (EC 2006)*[63] Put differently, the UK interpretation of radicalisation is largely contained in the current Prevent agenda, which defines radicalisation as *'the process by which people come to support terrorism and violent extremism and, in some cases, to then participate in terrorist groups. There is no obvious profile of a person likely to become involved in extremism or a single indicator of when a person might move to adopt violence in support of extremist ideas'* thereby suggesting that *'radicalisation is a process and not an event'* and that *'a gradual process is a fundamental component of radicalisation'*[64] (Home Office). Brian Jenkins (2007), terrorism and counterinsurgency expert at RAND, even refers to radicalisation as, *'the mental prerequisites to recruitment'*. In other words, 'there is no recruitment without radicalisation'. Again, the use of violence prevails in these definitions. Unimpressed, some have repeatedly voiced that radicalisation that leads to violence has been happening as far as we can gather. Dr Tim Stevens from the department of War Studies Kings College, London, has stressed that radicalisation in Britain is nothing new. On this point he informs us that *'There's always risk, radicalising the R word is nothing new, people have been radicalised into violence for as long as human kind has been around.'* For for the many social work and child-focused professionals entering or working on extremism agendas, I presume, these concepts are relatively new.

Many have attempted to distinguish terms, stating that *'although every*

---

62   Dutch intelligence service - AVID.

63   European Council definition on radicalisation.

64   Home Office - Contest Strategy.

terrorist is a radical, not all radicals are terrorists'. This implies that the radicali-sation process can evolve in all directions, including non-violent ones. Radicals and extremists can engage in non-violent behaviour without terrorist intent. By proposing that there might not be such a thing as a 'typical extremist' and those involved in extremism come from a range of backgrounds, requires further exploration. The research and evidence base pertaining to this risk group is limited, but is developing rapidly. Most individuals, even those who hold extreme views in a general sense, do not become involved in violence. Continuing on the notion of violent behaviour, and not forgetting that violent behaviour can operate on many levels in the absence of protective factors (such as poor reasoning skills) it is here, that children and young people will largely act within the context of their environment. This deserves considera-tion and is explored later on.

The argument is well settled and our analysis suggests that given the reasons set forth, extremists that are driven by violent views seek to generate interest and to provoke individuals towards engaging in acts of violence, and that the general consensus of all definitions arrives at a conclusion in our study, that the radicalisation of vulnerable individuals in this sense, is a deter-minative factor that in my view 'houses the use of violence on the founda-tion of extreme views that can occupy acts of terrorism'. Hence, the risk to children and young people are both enlarged and overwhelming in this sense. The inter-connectedness of these definitions arrives to other's philosophical and syntactical conclusions. This suggests that radicalisation is a journey that involves *'a process'* that can incorporate the *'physical use of violence'* and does not *'happen overnight'*. Taking this view into account, radicalisation is both a 'journey and process' which has 'destinations', radicalisation expert Dr Jonathan Githens-Mazer urges us to consider that *'Radicalisation is not limited'.* He elaborates by informing us that, *'we are part of the UK and this is a problem for everyone in the UK. In this day and age of technology which knows no bounds, we can't expect radicalisation to be limited to one area or another, I hope it not a growing trend, but it is not something that is going to go away'.* This leads to the question of identifying extremists, or even terrorists. Briefly, just to remind readers, it was the July 7th bombers that would inform us that the profiling of a typical extremist, is also problematic, given those involved in the London attacks were blended in mainstream society with respectable occupa-tions, which is a problem that is largely recognised by the British govern-ment and security service MI5. On this point the House of Commons report (2006) into the events after the London bombings, emphasised that, *'What we know of previous extremists in the UK shows that there is not a consistent profile to help identify who may be vulnerable to radicalisation' (Home office, 2005:31)*[65]. In short; there is not a typical profile of a terrorist or extremist. To conclude on this point, there is no single explanation for radicalisation and there are multiple factors at play. A more thorough account can be read in *'causal factors in radicalisation'* published in 2008 by Transnational Terrorism, Security and Law.

The problem of radicalisation of children and young people is not unique, but widely shared. Security experts in Australia have warned of children becoming radicalised there. Studies showed that the characteristics of Australians arrested in connection with jihadist activity tend to be young, with two-thirds under the age of 30 and 62% having not completed high school. Moreover, radicalised Australian children as young as six, have been shown calling for an end to democracy and Australia's way of life in a shocking extremist video. Four children, reportedly aged 6 to 13, claim that they want American President Barack Obama to go to hell and chant *'O Bashar we want your head',* referring to Syrian President Bashar al-Assad, in a video that was unearthed by Channel Seven. The disturbing footage was filmed at an event held by The Muslim Youth Project and is thought to have happened in December 2013.

CAUSES OF RADICALISATION

Agreeing the causes and drivers of radicalisations is often complex, contentious and at the same time obvious. However, we shall cover some of the common causes, which for social work and child care professionals will have considerable relevance for practice and for prevention. This knowledge will help towards structuring responses, assessments and interventions.

It has been noted that general assumption about the phenomenon of radicalisation leading to modern-day terrorism can be dated back as far as the 1960s and 1970s according to research. Correspondingly, some studies in the early 90s explored Muslims living in Europe who were under threat of radicalisation and attempted to unpack these issues further. The terrorist attacks in 2005 certainly put the 'icing on the cake', providing further comprehension and clarification. This brought some assumptions and speculations on the drivers and triggers of terrorism towards foreclosures, opening up others in the process. This unveiled a wealth of information that helped to address and approach the issues and complexities of home-grown terrorism more broadly.

---

65 Home Office: Prevent Strategy 2011.

Initially shrouded in mystique, however, were the questions of how and by whom?

According to research, the question of what causes radicalisation, both past and present, has generally included the following: relative depravation, alienation, western occupation and support for oppressive regimes, socio-economic integration, identity and politics, feelings of humiliation, marginalisation, discrimination or some other or social mechanisms. In dissecting some of these analytically, it will shed light and lead us towards understanding some of the indistinguishable efforts and methods deployed by extremists to recruit vulnerable individuals. It is here that I also propose that some other medical or related conditions could be the reasons behind these causes. These are expounded upon later on. These causes can be complex, profound and unmeasurable. For example, in terms of complexities, violent extremists and terrorists influence children and young people to engage and interact in behaviour driven by an ideology which causes them to engage in acts beyond their own human 'capabilities'. This can create or lead to some 'persistent adverse effect' on their well-being and overall condition. By doing so, it is the child and young person's emotional health and development that will be seriously damaged.

In light of the multiple causes (which cannot be possibly covered in this book) the urge and curiosity of children and young people to explore these and other issues that directly affect them could not be curtailed. In selecting one example such as identity and with reference to generations of young people growing up in the UK have experienced direct conflicts with values that traditionally, have been taught by their parents. These opposing values mature during transition from adolescence to adulthood, and become taxing and problematic. These conflicts, transitions and complexities have caused some young people to embark upon quests to search for new meanings and experiences to address these issues. A point that is well documented and noted by psychologist Paul A. Singh, in his reference to research conducted with Asian young people living in the UK, *Asian adolescents in the west*. He informs us that by the age of 14, young people will begin to ask these particular and other related questions. In avoiding generalisations, these questions are related to complex issues such as identity and sense of belonging. Because of these anxieties this has driven many towards confronting direct questions. These revolve around 'who am I?' and 'what sort of person would I like to be?'[66] This period of questioning, has also been described during the early

---

66   Asian Adolescents in the West, Paul A Singh, 1999.

1950s by an influential psychologist Erik Erikson. In his most famous publication 'Childhood and Society', Erikson describes this period:

A mature sense of identity means a sense of being at one with oneself as one grows and develops; and it means, at the same time, a sense of affinity with a community's sense of being at one with its future as well as its history or mythology'. (Erikson, 1974 pages 27 and 28)[67]

A more modern treatment of identity has been expounded upon by academics and practitioners, one being Dr Sangeeta Soni. She emphasises that the emerging themes of human expansion are inter-connected, in that '*the notion of identity is inextricably linked with our self-image'.* This invites other questions. For example, it is during these transitions, processes and complexities that extremists can seriously influence young people by offering alternatives or solutions in the form of a 'global religious identity' or even 'image'. It is here where we can draw some parallels from 7/7 in terms of identity. We question, did the July 7th bombers see themselves as 'British Muslims' or just 'Muslims'? Where they concerned that their Islamic identity was at risk of compromise and pressure from western contamination and did this accelerate their radicalisation? The co-founder of the Quilliam Foundation and one of Britain's high profile ex-Islamist extremists, Majid Nawaz says of himself at the start of his radicalisation process, '*feeling totally rejected by mainstream society, we were looking for an alternative identity'.* It is on the same line of reasoning that children and young people tend to explore their own inner feelings and views. This journey can accelerate them to exercise independent thinking with a navigation that is set towards exploring and searching for answers to unresolved conflicts and inherent complexities. In this sense, the search for a 'new or global identity' can become an operative agent towards radicalisation. This has been clearly demonstrated by the Islamic extremist group ISIS, who have offered these 'new identities' in exchange for engagement in violent jihad, which from our discussions in chapter two, is evidence of this powerful exchange currently being embraced by young people. This was a point well raised by the head of OSCT (Office Security Counter-Terrorism) Charles Farr to the Home office select committee in 2010. He informs them that, '*radicalisation seems to be reflected to a crisis in identity, to feeling of not being accepted or belonging'.* We must also conform to the line of reasoning presented by social psychologists. This suggests that many people in life tend to seek for a sense of belonging and sense of purpose, which for the reasons of fulfilment and self-actualisation, are clear motivations towards social change. However,

---

67   Working with diversity in youth and community work S Soni, 2010.

it is where these motivations lead them that is cause for alarm.

Continuing on this theme, and referring to young people in particular, some having already engaged in range inappropriate activities and behaviours, has triggered a process that has enabled them to change their personality and image. It is precisely because of these types of negative encounters, that young people are radically transformed with new identities and status. For example, those who were once law-abiding citizens given the social or economic conditions, such as poverty, can quite easily be coached towards engaging in criminal activity as a response to make ends meet. Simultaneously, distinct patterns have been seen with the pressures of youth and marginalisation. Because of this, it has driven young people to gravitate towards gang and gang culture. This in turn, creates a new sense of belonging, self-image and identity. In the same vein, extremists (having already altered their own self-image) have transformed themselves and have capitalised on the aforementioned discourses, offering alternatives to many young people in efforts to answer some of the diverse and complex questions and problems facing them today. It is in the same breath, that current services are unable to cope with extremist operations and subtle linguistics. In fact, for many delivering prevention work, the constraints of time, manpower or resources and particularly, where institutions are confined to working hours during the day and where extremists are operating exclusively outside of these conventional norms and realms, present additional and unforeseen challenges. This placed extremists at a clear advantage. Because of the aforementioned points and transitions, it has become more visible, that young people are now turning to religion to resolve life complexities and turn to the creator, God for divine guidance. This spiritual exchange has changed their identities in the process. For example, these assimilations are apparent for those intending to become Muslims who may be a 'revert' and for those intending to becoming Christians being 'born again'. In fact, to take it one step further, and in the words of one theologian, *'no one who reflects on life's ultimate questions can escape theology*[68]. It is also here as a professional practitioner that I postulate and stress that it is ludicrous to say or even suggest at this time, that young people have long abandoned religions as a means for survival or hope. On the contrary, many from a range of racial and cultural backgrounds have embraced its power, prestige and global appeal given the rapid rate of religious conversions worldwide, which for some have brought foreclosure to life's personal problems and complexities. This is evident in religions such as Islam seeing its growth worldwide

---

68 'Who needs Theology?' An invitation to the study of God (Grezen and Olson).

and Christianity, especially in countries such as India. This exchange has its benefits and in this sense, there are other factors at play that attract these individuals. For example, these types religions that have a global following, have the power to create new communities that can exclusively operate inside of realms not privileged to others. This also offers an organisational structure inside of these religious communities in which many can operate freely. These structures can be transitional (in a global community sense) and virtual. This is common and has been seen in Religion such as Islam. A popular term used by Muslims helps to reinforce this point. For example, 'Ummah' – denotes a community of believers which can be situated worldwide – this has a unique correlative aspect binding them together in the process. It is these types of structures and a sense of belonging to these communities that have appealed to many, especially young people, and is a selling point for extremists, especially amongst the disenfranchised. Professor Silke (2008) similarly points out that in many communities, 'joining a terrorist group increases the standing of a teenager or youth considerably.' He continues, 'It's also important to recognise the lure of danger and excitement, especially to young disenfranchised men'.

On the point of recruitment, extremists have clearly mastered the art of communication especially in 'the way they communicate' (given the many levels to the art of communication) as a powerful asset that has been incorporated into their deceptive quest to attract new recruits. Because of the overpowering presence of such profound, yet subtle information involved, it gradually opens up the listener making them warmer towards them and to actively seek out their company regardless of the setting. This creates the necessary opening where extremists can exploit and inject their violent and dangerous ideologies into the impressionable minds of children and young people. These openings have allowed extremist to take advantage of these opportunities. This approach has been captured and contextualised in a model developed by the Recora Institute, *'Recognising and Responding to Radicalisation; Considerations for policy and practice through the eyes of street level workers*[69]. This model offers insights and an explanation of how a person can come to internalise an ideology and the effects this can have on the vulnerable individual. This process has been termed by Recora as *'supply and demand'.* It supports the notion that there must be some 'cognitive opening' (a crisis which challenges previously held beliefs and assumptions) stemming

---

69   Recognising and Responding to Radicalisation; Considerations for policy and practice through the eyes of street level workers.

from some 'breeding ground' (trigger point – enables this ideology to become naturalised and universalised) that will enable the ideology to facilitate and nurture itself towards full-blown radicalisation through this process. It is here that a range of factors are discussed and further recommended reading is given through their website. I must inform the readers that recruitment can occur at different levels, which according to research, have been categorised as; external, social and individual. By applying the Recora model, we will establish that it equips professionals with a locus of understanding that will empower them more confidently to counter extremism and could prove useful within a number of ways. For example, for those working with children and young people, this will help to apply a range of interventions that may incorporate the following; early prevention, group work, formal and informal education, mentoring or therapeutic approaches. The vibrancy and flexibility of this particular model is fostered in its capacity to accommodate the many forms of extremism whether Islamic, Sikhism or Christian. Others include XRW and far-right groups. I must also stress that; hidden agendas of extremists are often expressed by the manifestation of the act of extremism during deliberation and not always prior to this in terms of build-up, as some have routinely believed. Because of this, the expertise of the workers is therefore required to be even more vigilant and diligent recognising these 'cognitive openings' and in reading signs and patterns. We must also distinguish behaviours that are loaded with high levels of aggression but are not driven by any extreme view or ideology.

For those working with children and young people in particular controlled settings, we must also consider the classification of behaviours that have been diagnosed and that have summoned us to consider the emotional and psychological effects of these behaviours that are contributory towards triggering their aggressive, and at times, violent behaviour. These have their origins. Some of these behaviours have been clinically diagnosed and referred to as conditions such as ADHD (Attention Deficit Hyperactive Disorder) and ASD (Autistic Spectrum Disorder), which for the purpose of this chapter have some relevance. What is highly significant here is, and it is often overlooked, that these particular conditions have been rife in influencing a range of feelings and behaviours for many years and may not be intrinsically driven by any 'extreme view' but are attributed to a lack of regulation on the individual's part to manage and channel their emotions in a positive way. This compartmentalises these as not sufficiently possessing the requirements to evolve into violent extremism or terrorism, with the majority of these conditions often monitored, regulated and managed through the use of therapeutic interventions or medication. On the other hand, however, given the age, such a diagnosis and condition could provide the openings for recruitment (as discussed in chapter one) towards extremism and which could raise the prospect of radicalisation considerably. This is demonstrated in the case studies later on. The ability to critically analyse is also a vital part of providing security. In taking this point on board, provides a more elaborate position towards understanding the role of protective factors that help to protect children and young people from danger. This is more difficult in understanding or seeing its relevance to preventing extremism. This requires some attention.

At best, children in particular, lack the ability to 'deeply analyse' large volumes of information, and the presence of powerful narratives, which incorporate profound and complex pieces of information, can be overwhelming. This can also be overpowering, rendering the child's intellectual ability to process such information ineffective. On the other hand, the ability to think critically and analyse, may enhance the child's or the young person's prospect of processing and interpreting information more accurately and safely, only if these skills are indelibly present. These analytical skills can delay or disrupt extremists' plans, especially in terms of recruitment, a point raised by one of it advocates, Dr Brooke Roger, a senior lecturer at Kings College, London, and a trained social psychologist. She emphasises that, '*if you give young people the critical thinking skills in the first place they will be less vulnerable to extreme views*'. These skills are acquired over the early years of a child's development and shape the way forward that will enable many professionals to educate children to distinguish behaviours that are associated or accompanied by the express use of violence. This is a valuable asset to this process and especially towards developing coping mechanisms that can help towards preventing violent extremism in the long-run. Because of this, they can challenge negative experiences that promote the direct use of negative behaviour as a means to respond or alter conditions. This enriches their ability to mobilise positive defences, thus positing protective factors in the process. This can also help to build up resilience.

According to the world-renowned psychiatrist and psychologist Sigmund Freud, he has often referred to the human psyche (personality) in terms of having distinct and profound aspects to its composition that needs to be protected. One key aspect he terms as the 'ego', that works by reasoning based on a 'reality principle' requires this greater protection from external and internal threats and dangers that could result in severe consequences to the individuals personality and behaviour, is by deploying what he has termed as 'defence mechanism'. It is these defense mechanisms that can help protect the person from danger, providing the necessary protective factors required to guard against dangers and to help promote a more healthy and safer ego. It is also the ego which governs or decides the way we behave or act, and where we must occupy ourselves to guard against the use of violence or influence towards violence. On this point, the lack of defenses or protective factors in children and young people can also be devastating and can open wide the door to a range of aggressive or violent behaviours. For example, we are reminded that those responsible for the death of child James Bulger in 1993 were inspired due to having watched violent scenes of Child Play 3 on television prior to killing the boy. It was his death that resulted in major legal overhaul which saw the age of criminal responsibility being drastically lowered to 10 years old. This raises serious questions about the psychological and pathological effects that violence has on vulnerable children and young people. This raises similar questions pertaining to the visual perceptions of children and young people that have observed acts of violence in a magnitude and intensity such as 9/11 and 7/7.

We are also informed by Freud that a term frequently used, that advocates these negative exchanges, 'reaction formation' describes the notion in which you can become extremely opposed to an idea or aspect of yourself that you are unwilling to accept. This can result in conflict. This reminds us of one of our examples discussed earlier in respect to identity and the independent thinking of children and young people that oppose parental values. This then, could have the potential to establish or trigger a process towards becoming violent or in our case, towards radicalisation, especially, if conflicts are left unresolved and at the discretion of extremists to exploit, foster and re-direct. Other theories, in terms of children's emotional and social development must be considered here. For example, lessons learnt from 'attachment theory' could provide a source of early identification and given the two distinct forms, 'secure' and 'insecure attachment', provide some insight, in terms of stable and unstable growth patterns. Children who experience 'insecure attachments' are at best to display contradictory behaviour and may, later, be attracted towards a role model outside of their own family circles to find some security. In this sense, extremists could offer these reassurances and securities. On the other hand, those children with 'secure attachments' will benefit extensively from the degree of warmth and are able to cope with new experiences better, often referring back to those encounters from their childhood as having positive impact on their lives often with less trauma.

Given these imperatives, children's socio-psycho development from western and eastern countries, vary dramatically. This implies that children from countries where extensive conflict is somewhat the 'norm' will have their belief systems influenced and nurtured in these war zones and will clearly accelerate towards radicalisation more rapidly than those from in non-war zones. In some cases children as young as five years old have been seen to become younger 'freedom fighters' (as showcased on BBC Panorama televised in October 2014)[70] and that any form of 'secure attachment' or even 'protective factors' will become nullified, rendering the child vulnerable and at risk of extensive harm. Because of this, we are informed that in a place like Iraq, insurgent groups have been accused of paying between US$50 to US$100 to teenagers to plant an Improvised Explosive Device (IED) to shoot a mortar or fire a machine gun at coalition troops. Though young, these teenagers have proved to be not only a dangerous threat but a security dilemma to the coalition forces. Given these views, it is painful to learn from Peter Singer's book *Children at War* that 300,000 children, both boys and girls, under the age of 18 are combatants fighting in almost 75 per cent of the world's conflicts. It is equally frightening to note that 80 per cent of these conflicts where children are present include fighters under the age of 15 and approximately 40 per cent of the armed organisations in the world (157 of 366) use child soldiers.

The need to inform and to educate a wide range of professionals is integral and fundamental to countering extremism as is the need to raise awareness in the minds of children and young people to these risks. By doing so, it will help to establish distinct processes in which these learnings will benefit them in multiple ways. For example, this may help to establish some of the following; overcoming one's own ignorance, reducing the level of risk through developing protective factors and in turn reducing their vulnerability to violence or even radicalisation. This in prevention terms, can barricade some of the channels, if not all of them, where extremists have attempted to indoctrinate children. Hence, the popular saying that *'knowledge is power'* presents itself here, to which I add *'a power that can defeat or prevent extremism'*. At the same time, it is necessary to visit theoretical perspectives that will help to distinguish and inform us of some of the following processes revolving around how children and young people are recruited, and to look at some of the factors used in and

---

70   BBC Panorama aired in October 2014.

towards recruitment. We shall consider some in brief, which have also been identified within counter-terrorism responses such as Prevent.

THEORETICAL APPROACHES

We must bear in mind that some of the theoretical framework discussed below will provide valuable insight in attempting to explain some of the dynamics and processes involved that underpin the radicalisation of children and young people. These theoretical frameworks are designed to address the way that we can observe, respond and prevent children and young people becoming the victim of extremism. In light of this and for the purpose of this chapter I have considered a few, which in my estimation, are relevant to this study.

Social movement theories provide explanations in addressing group facilitation, processes and mobilisation. This theory, in particular, explores the notion of network of relationships, which can serve to facilitate mobilisation even before awareness of the grievances of a group becomes prominent. It also recognises the importance of group dynamics that play into the radicalisation process. Extensive studies have suggested that many young people find acceptance, power and a strong sense of belonging in these groups. By doing so, they tend to flourish in these environments, surrendering their will to the dominant figures of these groups. Examples of this type of authority are commonly seen in settings such as school, within gangs and in religious institutions. In this sense, extremist some sought to offer alternatives, by maintaining the position of authority and by addressing the youth problems by steering them away from ungodly activities, so termed by some religious extremist, such as criminality and anti-social behaviour at community level, thereby adopting a mentoring and befriending role in this process and offering alternatives such as religion as a more appropriate replacement to address these social and economic problems and disadvantages. This approach and replacement had positive appeal to young people. The current Prevent agenda has also recognised these social movements used by extremist as drivers towards recruitment and radicalisation. This is referred to point 5.23 in the prevent strategy. These social movements gave scope to empower extremists to form 'cell groups'. The purpose of these enclosed groups was to avoid detection and because of their secret locations and invitation to restricted meetings, would appeal to young people. These meetings are held in locations such as abandoned properties, local community settings and, ironically religious institutions. Having taken on board the exposition on social movement theories and the wider context this has, especially in a terms of leadership and obedience to this authority, as we have just described, it leads us to one of the significant aspects that is required towards gaining any form of respect and obedience. This is the individual's acceptance of a distinct 'ideology' within this hierarchy. On this point, those who are responsible for leading such groups are on powerful ground by virtue of '*it legitimises the authority of the person in charge and justifies following his or her directives*[71]. Because of this, some researchers have suggested for example, that the recruitment or grooming into a radical group, is likely to accelerate and intensify the process towards radicalisation and affirms the position of a single or multiple abstractions in this process. Psychological theories, however, have attempted to describe similar processes.

According to Randy Borum (2014) writing in *Behavioural Sciences and the Law*, a key psychological vulnerability of those drawn to extremism is their need to feel they belong. '*In radical movements and extremist groups, many prospective terrorists find not only a sense of meaning,*' he writes, '*but also a sense of belonging, connectedness and affiliation.*'[72] In the same vein, many people are introduced to extremist ideologies through close-knit groups of friends. Within small groups of this kind, a classic psychological effect known as 'risky shift' (or 'group polarisation') frequently occurs. This is the tendency for groups to arrive at more extreme positions than any individual members would have done on their own. Again, reminding readers what was discussed earlier that 'radicalisation is a process and not an event'.

In 2006, Dutch psychologists Meertens, Prins and Doosje came up with an extensive overview of psychological theories of radical behaviours. *Cognitive Dissonance* for example, refers to a psychological phenomenon that emerges when people's behaviour is in conflict with their attitude and beliefs. One of the typical responses to such discomfort is that people increasingly start believing what they say. For example, most of us are well aware that children are commonly noted for expressing their educational and social aspirations or ambitions for example, 'when I grow up I would like to be a singer, doctor or actor' and would seem acceptable to many parents and professionals, especially in terms encouraging them to peruse these ambitions. On the flip side, statements such as, 'when I grow up I want to be a terrorist' sit in distinct isolation outside of everyday child vocabulary and would clearly suggest if this is perused, especially by extremist influences, will have devastating consequences, not just to themselves but also to others. It also here that I suggest, that for those professionals or even parents, what might not be clear in conversation

---

71   Hilgard's introduction to psychology, page 657.

72   Behavioural sciences and the Law.

at the time, could become clearer in their actions, and therefore any distinct behavioral signs or pattern must be taken seriously especially if such is loaded with violent expressions. The use of a person's observation can play an important role in prevention terms. Applying models such as 'situational literacy' has some relevance in this sense, which fundamentally argues it is what you read from a particular situation that can determine your next course of action, which can also determine possible intervention or even referral for disturbing behaviour. Biological theories have provided some interesting insight on this developing issue.

Professor Majid Ashy, Associate Professor of Psychology at Marrimack College and a research fellow on the development of bio-psychiatry in Saudi Arabia, persuades many to consider research that would suggest whether extremism is *'biologically based in the brain'*. The links between extreme faiths and mental health are developing. The former President of the Royal College of Psychiatrists Dr Dinesh Bhugra, has highlighted recent religious conversions as being more associated with a developing psychotic mental illness. In a paper entitled *Self-concept: Psychosis and attraction of new religious movements*, he points to data from studies which show that patients with first onset psychosis are likely to change their religion. Clearly, an alarming matter for the majority of children and young people diagnosed with severer prevailing mental conditions. Moreover, clinical research suggests that, *'radicalisation should be treated as a health issue in the same way as drugs and abuse, and that many youths are suffering from youthful naïveté'* [73] according to Kamaldeep Bhui, Professor of cultural psychiatry and epidemiology at Queen Mary University, London. Accordingly, we must also explore the developing medical concerns and their symptoms in light of neurotic drivers to radicalisation.

Religious fundamentalism and cruelty to children may one day be treated in the same way as mental illness, according to a neuroscientist. Kathleen Taylor, a research scientist at Oxford University's Department of Physiology, Anatomy and Genetics, says strong negative beliefs could be eradicated using techniques already in the works. Dr Taylor was speaking at the Hay Literary Festival in Wales when she was asked what she foresaw as positive developments in neuroscience in the coming years. She replied: *'One man's positive can be another man's negative. One of the surprises may be to see people with certain beliefs as people who can be treated. Someone who has for example become radicalised to a cult ideology...we might stop seeing that as a personal choice that they have chosen as a result of pure free will and may start treating it as some*

---

73   Professor Kamaldeep Bhui, Queen Mary University, London.

kind of mental disturbance. In many ways it could be a very positive thing because there are no doubt beliefs in our society that do a heck of a lot of damage. I am not just talking about the obvious candidates like radical Islam or some of the more extreme cults. I am talking about things like the belief that it is OK to beat your children. These beliefs are very harmful but are not normally categorised as mental illness.'

Briefly borrowing from criminological research, work with persistent offenders suggests that young people possess higher levels of impulsivity, confidence and risk-taking that play a vital role in attracting them towards 'new heights of actualisation'. In this sense, the glamorisation and sensation of the use of violence in religion to bring justice, appeals. Other arguments, such as the pathological factors as drivers towards radicalisation, must also be considered here. These argue that children and young people are pulled by forces beyond their own control, thus becoming agents of new social habits and behaviours that have the potential to be pull them towards extremism. I must also stress here, that professionals working with children and young people must, therefore, consider the contributions and interpretations offered by children and young people on subjects such as; terrorism, violence, martyrdom, 9/11, 7/7 and jihadism, as providing some early indication to determine and assess the potential for recruitment. More importantly, from a practice point of view, I would argue that we must not ignore the fact that some young people have sympathised with extremists, stressing they are defending 'just causes' and in doing so, have elevated them on a social, religious and international platform. These perceptions also have their origins, and are shaped during early childhood development. This can influence how they view and perceive individuals as good or bad, even if they are extremist, especially if they appear or seem to be standing up against injustice through the positive medium of religion.

In terms of illustrations, apparent examples are often seen within children's films. It is here where such concepts, views and perceptions are formed during early childhood. For example, a child favourite hero is often portrayed as the ultimate answer to eliminating evil. These have been seen with figures such as 'Iron man, Superman and Batman' with my favourite being Batman! Within these concepts, the conflict between 'good' v 'evil' helps to distinguish each other apart. On this basis, there is a separation in the form of 'them v us'. The distinctions, analogies and use of persuasive terms, are popular methods used by extremist and they are influential strategies used to recruit vulnerable individuals. The appeal of a superior figure, in this instance being God, who conflicts with a lesser opposing figure such as the devil clearly exemplifies the notion of 'good v evil' in religious conflicts. There is an essential linkage in this useful, yet, subtle template, demonstrated here, which encourages religious separation to the advantage of recruitment. Extremists, in adopting such a template, have attempted to master this persuasive narrative by installing 'theological and religious arguments' within this context. Inquisitive of these narratives, many have taken delight in admonishing and adopted these alternatives. In summarising, it could be argued that some of theories we have discussed, have all described one common denominator, and that is, extremists and terrorists have the potential to bring 'like-minded people together'. To reiterate again, examples were apparent with the July 7th bombers, whose connections with known extremists prior to the London attacks, were linked outside of the UK and were known to MI5. It is here that I must stress, that this rapidly emerging phenomenon called 'radicalisation'-has been operative for many years. This implies that its origin has some historical significance.

HISTORICAL ROOT TO RADICALISATION

Extremists and terrorists in particular, have chosen to delve more deeply into their views to ensure, as discussed earlier, that good prevails against evil, even if this evil must be eliminated in the form of suicide campaigns. Resultantly then, a comprehensive analysis of this struggle between good v evil in this context must be launched. For example, according to Payne in 2009, he found that the Al-Qaeda narrative is characterised by the concepts of Islamic utopia, an 'us' versus 'them' dichotomy. By contrast, government narratives were also characterised by these concepts in efforts to undermine terrorist groups such as Al-Qaeda and to build resilience and community cohesion through a sense of 'Britishness'. However, this counter-response was problematic for a range of reasons, some that were hypocritical, impossible of being achieved or even co-existing. A clear distinction of this challenge can be seen within our current society. British values and social practices are at times in direct conflict to religious ones, and again children and young people were often caught between these two camps. For example, the use of alcohol, tobacco, promoting sexual practices and the legalisation of drugs are viewed as immoral and evil and are strictly forbidden practices within most world religions today such as Judaism, Christianity, Islam and Sikhism and in this sense, are therefore are subject to 'conflict'. This is perceived, by religious extremist and terrorist groups such as AQ and ISIS, as an attempt by western governments, given these liberal laws that promoted such practices that were supported by western governments and one that encouraged many towards becoming secularised, including young people, as direct attack against religion. Because of these temptations to transform individuals and subtle attempts to fragment religion, it has been viewed by many that religion has been perceived as the guardian of humanity, especially against such temptations and a shelter from the compromises of life. This granted religious extremists, many acting as guardians of these religions that were at risk of secularisation, even more weight and a platform to enforce their messages more unreservedly in desperate attempts to challenge these ungodly practices against those systems that promoted such lifestyles. In fact, the acts of extremists in defending religious positions sought to generate the view that the use of violence was sanctioned by God in these particular circumstances, especially were the risk of a religion that was established by God was threatened from these systems or governments and one that enforced this position with greater conviction in efforts to eradicate this evil system. Given these religious differentiations, one prominent figure responsible for the radicalisation of many through this route of campaigning against such immorality, was an Egyptian man, Islamic theorist, Journalist, author and a leading member of the Egyptian Muslim brotherhood, called Syyd Qutb.

It was during the early 1950s that Qutb sought to justify the unanimous use of violent jihad by unequivocally challenging the systems that opposed God. Aspects of his convictions stemmed from his moral encounters during his short stay in America. Having experienced and observed, first hand, the moral and religious decline of western society and values, which would give Islam, in his view, a central position towards restoring humanity's decline. This persuaded him that democracy (as a system) sought to indoctrinate, secularise and conform individuals to engage in ungodly practices that were in direct conflict and contradistinction with the very character of God, whereas on the other hand, religion sought to liberate. The system he described has been in existence, during the time of the prophet Muhammad and arguably, even hundreds of years earlier. It has commonly been referred in Arabic as 'Jahiliyah' (describing the powers that are in authority).

This system possessed the capability of transforming people through its social, materialistic and political appeal and possessing the authority to 'flaunt' its status, especially within western countries, and others countries that were susceptible to its glamorisation. This led to conflicts, contentions and confrontations, some that have been happening for thousands of years.

Similarities are apparent in the Old and New Testaments, particularly with the Hebrew prophet Moses and the Messiah Jesus Christ. Their encounters against these systems resulted in excessive violence and large scale confrontations. These were applicable with Moses against Pharaoh in Egypt and Jesus Christ against the Roman Empire. This is intended to replicate itself, according to Biblical prophecies, surrounding the second coming of Jesus Christ to his place of nativity in Jerusalem, on this occasion to reign as mortal king[74]. For a more comprehensive and detailed analysis readers are advised to consult leading experts and scholars in this field. It is also here that the contribution of a functionalist sociologist view of religion as a means to promote change is a critical factor towards maintaining social harmony and social integration, which is where extremists could argue these discourses. According to one of the most famous sociologists, Emile Durkheim, *'religion was closely related to the collective consciousness of society'*[75] even if society is becoming more *'complex through processes of modernisation which also serve to fulfil certain social functions'*[76] It was these functions, structural systems and inter-connectedness of religions that was at risk of evaporating because of the overwhelming power of secularisation and democracy and where religious extremists in particular sought to preserve and protect from these compromises.

On these grounds, Qutb's controversial narratives, were translated into tangible forms and were loaded with violent connotations. One of his most notable, and dangerous, publications, 'Ma'alim fial Tingu, termed, 'milestones' fundamentally argued that in order to preserve these religious values the use of violence was justified, especially in the form of applying offensive jihad where necessary. In this context of religion, he makes a clear distinction between groups, which predominately are situated in two camps, 'believers' and 'non-believers'. In promoting these views, Qutb would persuade believers to stand up against injustice and oppression from western governments by exercising violent jihad. In this sense, Qutb consents to the use of violent jihad within modern societies, chiefly, for reasons pertaining, *'to establish God's authority in the earth, to arrange human affairs according to the true guidance provided by God; to abolish all the satanic forces and satanic systems of life; to end lordship of one man over others.'* His narratives and publications were adopted by groups such as Al-Qaeda. Now armed with even more material, they would eventually remobilise their offences and enforce such a position against western democracy in favour of a more godly system.

The Prevent agenda would compartmentalise Qutb's views as 'disturbing'

---

74   New Testament (King James Versions) Holy Bible.

75   Emile Durkheim – and the collective consciousness of a society.

76   Emile Durkheim – and the collective consciousness of a society, study of Smith, K.

and 'far-fetched' further acknowledging that such possessed the capacity and the potential to radicalise vulnerable people in the UK towards engaging in violent acts and terrorism. Prevent protests and was adamant that Qutb did not allude to violent jihad against the west; rather that his interpretations have been misunderstood and taken out of context by terrorists in attempts to recruit people within the west, stressing the use or concept of jihad was pertaining to an 'individual personal struggle pertaining to life challenges' and not for the use of violence against others (Home Office 8: 11). The use of terrorism legislation would also provide sanctions and support the Prevent agenda, namely with respect to the Terrorism Act 2006 section 1 and 2 *publication or circulation of materials that glorified or supports the use of terrorism*[77]. The problem of radicalisation continues to raise debate and discussion.

In reference to these growing concerns, evidence presented to the Home Office select committee on the subject of radicalisation in 2012, was an opportunity for the Home Secretary Theresa May, to reassure the committee of their efforts and responsibility to safeguard the general public from extremism. The interrogation by the select committee (chaired by Keith Vaz) eventually culminated in a verbal exchange of questions and omission of information from the committee to those responsible. Explanations given by the Director-General of OSCT, Charles Farr, disclosed, amongst other things, their inability and certainly the impossibility of security services preventing individuals from becoming radicalised within in the UK. Others have informed the committee because of the terror attacks in 2005, this has given status and focus exclusive to Muslim community, which runs the risk of ignoring other communities with similar problems. On this point, Dr Inderjit Singh of the network of Sikh Organisations had informed the select committee in 2010 that, *'a sort of favoured status as a result of radicalisation'* suggesting some altercations were necessary to find a balance, yet, address the risks and threats presented to all of us. It was clearly unfolding that this was a problem beyond their existing resources and yet again, the quest to search for concrete solution, continued. Furthermore, as extremists gradually became more strategic in their operations and with a view to recruit individuals, kept security and intelligence services on their feet. Given current concerns, the committee would reconvene in July 2014, with the intention of questioning others on similar matters of radicalisation; this time it would be the interrogation of the Assistant Principal of Park View School in Small Heath, at the heart of what is widely known as the 'Trojan Horse plot', as previously discussed in chapter two.

---

77   The Terrorism Act 2006 – sections 1 and 2.

On the other hand, some have suggested that the radicalisation of children and young people in the UK could be fuelled by our own government. A report by Sky News in June 2014 by their social affairs and education editor, Afua Hirsvch, has contested the current government strategy, stating that social media is *'still fuelling Islamic extremism'*. The report stressed that the current government strategy of censoring and blocking terror-related content on the internet is not working, according to a new report. An in-depth study of people who support jihadist groups found that Facebook, Twitter and YouTube were still fuelling radicalisation. A report by counter-extremist think-tank Quilliam, criticised the government strategy of censorship and filtering, saying it was an ineffective, costly and counter-productive means of countering extremism, Dr Erin Marie Saltman, research project officer at Quilliam stating that, *'currently there's a large focus for governments to use censorship, blocking terror-related content'*. One former extremist who was radicalised as a teenager said *'more work was needed to address root causes of radicalisation'*. Social media creating the environment and providing a platform to flaunt extremist propaganda and material has caught the attention of many respondents. A conference held by Professor Barry Richards from Bournemouth University in 2011, has described this as a growing problem. On this point, Prof Richards notes that the problems are with, 'expanding digital networks' raising essential questions about the media role in *'fuelling the fear of the public perceptions of extremism'*. Dr Ben O'Loughlin from Royal Holloway has enforced this position emphasising that, *'it is the BBC, that's radicalising people.'* Taking it further, Professor Andrew Hoskins from the University of Glasgow points out that we keep the extremist messages in a *'new media of ecology'*. In attempts to analyse, explore and respond to the many avenues to radicalisation, the EU Commission launched the RAN (Radicalisation Awareness Network) in 2011. This consisted of 500 leading experts from member states tasked with countering violent extremism. A spokesman on the subject stressed that, *'The terrorist threat has somewhat shifted away from organised groups to individuals or loose and small cells, who are harder to detect and whose actions are harder to predict. To prevent further tragedies, we must adapt our counterterrorism capabilities to these new challenges. Our response must begin with a deeper understanding of the processes that lead to radicalisation.'*

CASE STUDIES

The obvious eventualities would be that casualties would emerge, points that have been raised from chapter one. The signs that children and young people were amongst those targeted and becoming radicalised, without any connection to any individual or group, alerted counter-terrorism officers' attention to explore the complexities surrounding the acceleration of this radicalisation process fuelled by the individuals themselves. This process has been termed as 'self-radicalisation'.Such notions began to chip away that young people sought to educate themselves on subjects of profound complexity; this also has it merits, but on the other hand, has its disadvantages. The quest for 'knowledge and understanding' certainly pricked the curiosity of individuals who resorted to isolate and withdraw themselves from the public domain to investigate these issues further. Initially, this prompted little suspicion. Those who were starved of these answers quickly made use of technology to feed themselves. This was equally as problematic for security services to monitor, as the role of social media as a virtual teacher, which, in these instances, would become an ideal tool for extremists to exploit. Certainly, this confirmed that the real concerns of extremism and terrorism had arrived comfortably within the homes of children and young people, without the formal presence of any person or group. This has generated another term used by some, as the 'new madrasas'. The threat of extremist using social media to gain recruits is running the risk of turning the UK into a 'social media graveyard'.

An interesting case of a young white British male formally known as Nicky Anthony Riley, attracts our attention to analyse the dynamics of recruitment and radicalisation, even more closely. His conversion to a radical form of Islam, resulted in him changing his name and identity to 'Mohammed Abdullah Azeem'. This exchange which was encouraged by religious extremists, led Abdullah to embrace what he had thought had been lacking for years and which he had conscientiously believed, he had found through his new found religion and so-called friends. Having already been diagnosed with an autistic spectrum condition and known to have seen a psychiatrist at the young age of 9, meant that he had a condition that was compatible with and contributory to his radicalisation and one that placed nicely into the hand of extremist. This set the stage for terrorist attack. This resulted in his attempts to blow up the Giraffe restaurant in Exeter in May 2008; though no loss of life occurred, casualties emerged and considerable damage was done to the venue and to himself. He would be later convicted of terrorism related offences and be sent to jail. Again, reminding us of the aforementioned theories of social process that can contribute towards a person's radicalisation by facilitating change, must be taken seriously in these and similar scenarios. It would not be until 7/7 that considerations were brought to the attention of services that factors such as 'withdrawal' or 'isolation' could become catalysts that could accelerate the radicalisation process and in recognition of this it would be taken more seriously, especially during risk assessments and observations. Over the last few years, this criterion has enlarged, incorporating a wider remit that highlights a range of vulnerabilities that is constantly emerging. This has also been embedded into current training that address the wider social, emotional and psychological conditions that can cause violent behaviour and radicalisation, because of these vulnerabilities. This has also been outlined in some of the following, section 11 of the Children Act 2004 and has also been used in PVE training which explores these risk factors, which is discussed in detail in chapter four.

Another highly intriguing case involving a young person would attract the attention of media, as it did numerous responses from professionals. The burning of a Qur'an in 2010, by a white female teenager within the Sandwell borough, certainly triggered concerns as it did hostility from the Muslim community. The young person, who was attending a local school at the time, gave rise for professionals, amongst other things, to respond to any safeguarding concerns. Having been involved within the operational responses to such an incident and through attending local meetings in attempts to explore effective strategies, it was problematic for the majority of the professionals involved, Prevent officers, racial equality representatives and youth workers. The wider implications of her actions were anticipated with fear and the local police were on high alert as the prospect of any revenge attack (from opposing communities or young people) was eagerly anticipated. This sought to contaminate community relations during the proceedings and further stigmatise Muslim. These observations have been cited in research conducted by Dr Chris Allen, who, in writing on the controversial subject of 'Islamophobia' is a notion to be deeply considered in these and similar events. This creates problems for reconciliation, especially for those Muslims who are sincere and genuine towards tackling extremism.

These examples were clear and lessons learnt from those responsible for the London July 7th Bombings, with particular reference to Siddique Khan, the oldest of four suicide bombers, may hold clues in helping to comprehend to what extent extremists will go to propagate their intentions even if this involves contact with children and young people. Khan had a good education and became interested in helping disadvantaged youngsters. He eventually took a job as a school youth worker, and at this point became serious about his faith. He told his associates he had turned to religion after a far from unblemished youth during which he had been involved in fights, drinking and drugs. Khan's resentment and grievances were targeted against the UK government and were further demonstrated in his covert actions. He would channel his negative emotions by constantly arguing the fact that the role of western powers in conflicts with the Muslim world was unacceptable, which further frustrated him. The outcome of his 'irrational reasoning' was to produce a home-grown terrorist. It would eventually become clearer that social networks (discussed earlier) had played a part in Khan's radicalisation, having previously attended Finsbury Park Mosque (where Abu Hamza-hook conducted public sermons), and spent time in numerous talks and discussions on topics such as religion and politics, including at his place of work.

I cannot stress enough, that the use of narratives as an appealing prospect must not be underestimated as one study has already explained that, *'some of the narratives, such as the call to martyrdom used to recruit children to the cause of jihad, strap lethal bombs on themselves in exchange for the promise of seventy two virgins and detonate bombs and their bodies in crowded public spaces because they are told that is what Allah demands, are evidence enough of the enduring lure of powerful narratives and their very real danger'.* There is a power that narratives have to alter perceptions of reality, to change minds, and to influence choices and actions, that must also be considered in terms of the psychological and social effects this can have on influencing children towards embracing extremism. In light of this I would remind readers that *'access creates opportunities'.* It is precisely because of these points, views and issues discussed in this chapter that Prevent would need to integrate itself more firmly into safeguarding environments and realms.

4: Safeguarding, a Prevent Approach

The aim of the Prevent strategy is to stop people becoming terrorists or supporting terrorism. Prevent is part of the Government's counter-terrorism strategy. It draws on counter-terrorism funding, in some cases legislation and on counter-terrorism resources.

Home Office: 6:1

The government response to terrorism in the UK was in the form of detailed strategic counter-terrorism strategy produced by the Home Office in 2003 entitled 'CONTEST'. The document outlined measures that would help to counter terrorism in the UK with a prime focus on 'preventing violent extremism'. Importantly, the strategy sought to educate the counter-terrorism community with an emphasis on raising the profile pertaining to the radicalisation of vulnerable individuals in the UK. In this sense, the strategy attempted to provide some respite from extremism and terrorism in the UK. This did not come without its opposition. It was expected that many were set to embrace this new agenda with 'open arms'. Nothing could have been further than the truth. As discussed in chapter one, the Prevent arm of the strategy would become the most applicable to a wide range of services and organisations working with children and young people. Prevents overall image lacked considerably in a number of ways. Topping the list was its aesthetic appeal. This needed a considerable 'make-over' and given what we often say 'first impressions last', Prevent has certainly lasted. I must point out to the readers that Prevent has undergone a series of reviews since its proliferation. These have been seen with CONTEST II introduced in 2009 and then the most recent version CONTEST III in 2011. Initially, prevent was the least developed out of the strategy.

The Prevent agenda had managed to gain a reputation that had, inadvertently labelled and singled out certain communities as the possible suspects. The most obvious being the Muslim community. This was in danger of reinforcing stereotypes and stigmas. Indeed, the advice from OSCT (Office of Security and Counter-Terrorism) that had forewarned many that the biggest threat to the UK will come from Al-Qaeda and Islamic inspired terrorism, though obvious due to the terrorist attacks on 9/11 and 7/7, was also perceived as a deliberate attempt to marginalise those from Muslim communities in efforts to identify suspects. This was clearly demonstrated with the less favourable treatment and injustices against the majority of Muslims (or Asians in general for that matter) both old and young within the UK post 9/11. Under increased pressure from terrorist movements in the UK the random use of terrorism legislation, in attempts to stop and locate suspects, has led to further negative experiences. This involved monitoring anyone that fitted the 'stereotypical image' of a terrorist, and again, an Asian male with a long beard was an ideal starting point. This ran the risk of giving sweeping generalisations about these groups. In the same vein, it was hardly surprising that the former Home Secretary John Reid, when coming to office, in his first public speech to a Muslim audience in East London - he called for Muslim parents '*to be on the lookout for tell-tale signs of extremism in their children*'.[78] This did not look good.

These and other abnormalities, in reference to the aforementioned legislation, were a result of the misuse and to some extent abuse of the Terrorism Act 2000 with reference to 'stop and search'. This gave credence to suspicions that governments took pride in inequality. This was a risk of damaging community relations. Moreover, this did not improve government standing; some taking it further by labelling governments as 'blatantly racist'. This did not stop here. Additional legislation introduced in 2005 imposed further sanctions. The terrorism Act 2005 saw the use of 'control order' come into force for the first time and was immediately used against known suspects living within local community to monitor and restrict their movements. Again these suspects were predominantly of Muslim origin. These have often been termed as another form of 'in-house arrest' and gave rise to opposing humanitarian groups, such as Liberty, to argue fundamental breaches of human rights not to mention discrimination. This raised security questions in the minds of the general public. The presence of suspected 'criminals' living in the local neighbourhood, especially related to or even charged with terrorism offences, left many nervous and anxious. Because of these and other discourses, the contribution from independent think-tanks, many of which unequivocally challenged government policy, suggested that a complete overhaul was needed to reassure the public and to act fairly in all cases where suspicion of extremism and terrorism were brought to light. This sought to redress the imbalances and eliminate the aforementioned stigmas. One report in particular, would have positive impact by challenging those in authority by creating a sense of direction away from convention.

---

78   Islamophobia – page 94, Ashgate, Dr Chris Allen.

In July 2013 the Home Affairs Select Committee launched an inquiry into counter-terrorism. This was focused on the 'Pursue' strand of CONTEST, which is deigned to stop terrorists. This followed on from the committee work on 'Prevent' in its inquiry into *the roots of violent radicalisation* in 2010. One recent report submitted to the Home Office Select Committee, by professor Aruni Kundai from 'Claystones' an independent research think-tank, entitled 'A decade lost, rethinking radicalisation and extremism' sought to 'iron out the creases'. His recommendations to the committee offered a fresh thematic analysis towards counter-extremism. Implying that a radical overhaul of Prevent was required and that a clearer defining of 'British Values' was necessary to alleviate any apprehensions imported or conceived. This was the impetus required that would invite reforms for the purpose of change and positive engagement. More pointedly, the facts contained in this report were not merely descriptive, but evidence of the sheer volume and range of views expressed, abstracted from a variety of sources, particularly pertaining to the wider challenges to counter-terrorism. Interestingly, the contents were acknowledged. These were cited by the Home Office Select Committee in their final publication in 2014 with reference to page 189 of the document, for providing some analysis to the challenges of extremism, which for Claystone's reputation and efforts, was a step in the right direction. Because of these issues raised, Britain was again under pressure to defend its reputation as a country of 'tolerance' though it was becoming clear in the atmosphere this was getting tougher and tougher.

In spite of the opinion polls regarding Prevent, prevention work has continued to receive financial and political backing since 7/7. There were inherent complexities and reservations with Prevent as the backlash from critics was becoming a regular occurrence. Professor Anthony Glees (an intelligence and security expert at the University of Buckingham) summarised this problem concerning Prevent, *'the problem now is with Prevent. It makes perfect sense to stop young Muslims from being seduced into extremism and violence, but the question of how we do it and who should do it has not been answered. The task to identify suitable applicants to deliver this agenda is endless*[79]. Despite the polemics of Prevent, it is necessary for those working with children and young people to understand that the Prevent agenda is the recommended approach to counter-terrorism within the UK and in this sense, as we have been discussing since chapter one, it is difficult to contest otherwise. On the other hand, Prevent, as a counter-terrorism measure, has also attracted

---

79   Professor Anthony Glees, University of Buckingham.

a wealth of fresh data which proved useful in a number of ways. At a macro level, Prevent provided the ideal environment, framework and springboard, particularly in terms of safeguarding, to explore key issues entirely in a new context. Crucially, this enabled professionals and practitioners the flexibility to construct templates, assessments and interventions that revolved around these new developments. Adding to this growing cluster of work, the use of random interventions over the years has been like 'a net which has been cast over the sea of extremism' in desperate attempts to capture some outcomes and conclusions. Surely a new emphasis was needed. Whilst Prevent has welcomed the many contributions from its participants, it is in the same breath that I postulate, that some of the interventions used, may have been conceived on a catalogue of assumptions. This emphasises even more so, that an effective and credible 'solution' is still warranted.

The fact that Prevent programmes are in regular review and subject to constant change, especially in terms of focus and delivery, convinces us that the search for 'exceptional responses' has been a journey often laden with casualties along the way. For the readers who may be bewildered and still unsure regarding 'what works' given the range of options that have already been preferred or suggested, uncertainty is often the conclusion. These uncertainties have also been contributed by 'Prevent students' as I term, who have conformed to and advocated its concepts, principles and objectives since 2006. This has also been interfered with and shaped by global events of terrorism. In spite of all this, the government is of the opinion, that Prevent has met its requirement to offer counter-terrorism measures, and the Home Secretary's statement about the current Prevent agenda (see below) is certainly suggestive of its accomplishment. Her condemnation of the previous Prevent agenda, however, was an attempt to persuade many to actively commit themselves to this newly revised version and abandon the previous government's over-enthusiastic promises that have significantly failed to address the task at hand.

Finally, in terms of compromise, the dependency on Prevent alone as a counter-terrorism measure has caused considerable pain largely for those with religious beliefs or affiliation. For example, the vast majority of Muslims working on these agendas (which have been numerous) argue the proposition that the religious conviction of Islam's followers is technically at risk, and for those employed on such agendas, the potential to compromise this position is readily available. It is within these types of opportunities that the actions of committed Muslims (or those committed to other faiths for that matter) to consciously and intentionally expose the 'dirty linen' of fellow Muslim brothers and sisters (irrespective of their legitimate views), has been tampered with by Prevent. These temptations have caused turmoil, compelling some to reconsider their position, while others have chosen to withdraw or even resign. This has affected not just those employed within the UK but also the wider international prevention community, influencing others (working on similar agendas) to incorporate tighter monitoring procedures again reinforcing stereotypes and stigmas. It is here that we shall expound upon the transition of safeguarding into Prevent.

PREVENT AGENDA

Since the London terror attacks, an estimated £45 million has been spent on 'preventing violent extremism' agenda, primarily through the DCLG (Department for Communities and Local Government). However, this figure rose to an estimated £140 million during 2008/2009 across a variety of organisations including; Home Office, DCLG, Foreign Office, and the then Department of Children, Schools and Families, now the DfE (Department for Education). Moreover, during 2008-2010 an estimated £3.5 million was allocated to the Youth Justice Board to share between Youth offending teams for the purpose of preventing violent extremism. Prevent also required monitoring. In this sense, its key performance and National Indicator was called the NI35. This focused on *Building Communities Resilience to Violent Extremism'*. Amongst its many functions its emphasised to those working on this agenda, as contained in this national indicator to consider the *'knowledge and understanding of the drivers and causes of violent extremism and the prevent objectives'.* I presume, for the many participants and supporters of Prevent, in profitability terms *'Prevent deposit has been well worth the investment'* over the years.

Prevention work (a familiar term nowadays) which denotes in a general sense, an *'action that stops something before it happens'* and for the purpose of this particular study it refers to steering children and young people away from *'a range of dangers and behaviours that are classified as presenting clear and present danger both to themselves and others',* could be suggested was another driving force and reason behind the Prevent agenda mobilisation. Since the July 7th London Bombings, the potential dangers and risk factors have enlarged. Increasingly then, prevention work has become a critical component in counter-terrorism work. The current head of counter-terrorism in the UK, Charles Farr, summed up the role of prevention strategies, stating:

'that much larger groups that feel a degree of negativity, if not hostility towards the state, country, the community, and who are, as it were, the pool in which terrorists can swim'.

I presume that Prevent intends to proselytise many more towards this direction. Prevent did not hold back from making its intentions clear, as part of rooting out those extremists that threatened the public and the values it has been built upon, directly referred to in the strategy as being distinctly 'British' or of British origin, and condemned anyone, let alone extremists, from threatening this precious edifice. This was also perceived as an offence. This deliberate statement in the strategy, as interpreted by some, was as a blatant disregard and exclusion of other cultures. This sought to regress many to their former logistical concepts and to former views. This was in danger of fuelling extremism. The use of the term 'British values' conjured up many thoughts and certainly put up some defences in the minds of many religious and non-religious individuals. Some naturally felt excluded. For those employed to deliver counter-terrorism work, these governmental constraints were worrying and many sought refuge elsewhere, gravitating towards other agendas, such as cohesion, in professional attempts to exercise their views more comfortably and to liberate themselves from the stigma of Prevent. Conflicts arose for those with religious, social and cultural values that opposed, contested or that were in contradistinction with British values. This begged other questions. The most popular, I gather: what does it mean to be British? In spite of these virulent discourse and repercussions, the Prevent agenda has remained undeterred on this position, as it has unreservedly defined extremism as:

'A vocal or active opposition to fundamental British Values, including democracy, the rule of law, individual liberty and mutual respect and tolerance of different faiths and belief Also included in extremism are calls for the death of members of the armed forces, whether in this country or overseas.' (Home Officer 2011:34)

Again, reminding us of the aforementioned report, which suggests that another impetus is needed. It has been repeatedly voiced that the Prevent agenda has attracted questions on its ability to deliver credible programmes of intervention. It was clear that the previous Prevent agenda (under Labour government) lacked consistency, accountability and focus, which caused us to arrive at the revised version in 2011. The previous agenda was paved with fundamental 'flaws' making it impossible at the time to capture any promising or prevailing programme of intervention as completely fulfilling the task at hand and as a template for others to adhere too. A range of inquisitions prompted further interrogation from political figures by putting those responsible for fostering Prevent's development and orientation 'in the dock'. Notwithstanding this, a House of Commons parliamentary debate in July

2014 aimed at Prevent was certainly an opportunity to expound on these views. Yvette Cooper (Labour MP for Normanton, Pontefract and Castleford) was less optimistic about the nostalgia of the current Prevent to complete the task. On this point, she asked the Home Secretary to make a statement on her conduct regarding the Government's action on preventing extremism. The Home Secretary Theresa May would respond, in a most challenging tone and with a lengthy explanation, stressing:

'*The Government takes the threat of extremism—non-violent extremism as well as violent extremism—very seriously. That is why, in line with the Prime Minister's Munich speech in 2011, I reformed the Prevent strategy that year, and it is why, in response to the killing of Drummer Lee Rigby, the Prime Minister established the extremism taskforce last year, the Prevent strategy we inherited was deeply flawed. It confused Government policy to promote integration with Government policy to prevent terrorism. It failed to tackle the extremist ideology that undermines the cohesion of our society and inspires would-be terrorists to murder. In trying to reach those at risk of radicalisation, funding sometimes reached the very extremist organisations that Prevent should have been confronting. Ministers and officials sometimes engaged with, and therefore leant legitimacy to, organisations and people with extremist agendas*.' She continues, '*Under this Government, foreign hate preachers such as Zakir Naik and Yusuf al-Qaradawi are banned from coming to Britain. Under her Government, they were allowed to come here to give lectures and sermons, and to spread their hateful beliefs. In the case of al-Qaradawi, he was not just allowed to come here; he was literally embraced on stage by Labour's London Mayor, Ken Livingstone*.' She continues, '*I have excluded more foreign hate preachers than any Home Secretary before me. I have got rid of the likes of Abu Hamza and Abu Qatada. The Government do not give a public platform to groups that condone, or fail to distance themselves from, extremism. For the first time, we are mapping out extremists and extremist groups in the United Kingdom*'

In persuading us of the whys, not so much the hows, the Home Secretary's comments, nevertheless, proved influential. Crucially, her important view sums up the distinctive features of the current Prevent agenda which were summarised in the following: '*Prevent is part of the UK counter-terrorism strategy and aims to reduce the number of people becoming or supporting violent extremists. Prevent happens before any criminal activity takes place. It is about recognising, supporting and protecting people who might be susceptible to radicalisation*.' This then leads us to elaborate on the Prevent objectives.

There are currently three key Prevent objectives outlined within the revised

Prevent Strategy published in 2011. These are as follows (note: these may change with the pending general election of government scheduled for May 2015, if further reviews are commissioned)

Objective 1. Ideology - respond to the ideological challenge of terrorism and the threat we face from those who promote it.

Objective 2. Individuals - prevent people from being drawn into terrorism and ensure that they are given appropriate advice and support.

Objective 3. Institutions - work with sectors and institutions where there are risks of radicalisation which we need to address.

The revised Prevent strategy has maintained its position to peruse any form of extremism that lead towards terrorism or support the use of terrorism, so stating that, *'Prevent will continue to deal with extremism where it is shown to be conducive to terrorism'.* Building on these insights, the current Prevent agenda has focused its attention on priority sectors. These would be narrowed down to the following: education, faith, criminal justice, health and charities[80]. In parallel with this, it deliberately selected boroughs across the UK, for obvious reasons, that would receive Prevent funding; especially those that were considered *'hotbeds for extremism growth, recruitment and radicalisation'.* In recognition of this, the Prevent agenda attempted to deprive terrorists of new recruits. It is here that I postulate, almost ten years since the London terrorist attacks in 2005, that Prevent is on a route to exist alongside, if not exceed, most agendas where the concerns to safeguard children and young people are a major component to their work. Needless to say, other problems have stalled this process since 2005.

The need to inform a wide and diverse range of professionals on a range of terrorism issues was integral to Prevent's success. For example, fast tracking professionals through a coherent education on extremism and terrorism was quite demanding and at times, proved counter-intuitive. In fact, every professional that was desirous of constructing an effective foundation to counter extremism and safeguard children and young people in the process, would have to make substantial use of the principles, frameworks, systems and contents on both safeguarding and the Prevent agenda. To go one step further, one could not engage effectively without understanding or referring to the other. These rectifications, along with a whole range of other views, were resident prior, during and long after the Prevent consultation in 2010. We shall briefly discuss these.

Overall, 11 consultation events took place around the UK with an

---

80   HM Prevent Strategy point 3.37.

estimated 600 people in attendance. Having attended the last Prevent review consultation held in Birmingham in December 2010, opportunities arose to ask direct questions. By doing so, the information from respondents, helped to navigate the Prevent agenda towards better outcomes (given the purpose of the consultation was such) and the notion of an inter-agency approach to tackling extremism outside of standard conventions, was certainly a promising venture especially for Prevent's future success, points that are better reserved for discussion in chapter five. Those in the driving seat and responsible for Prevent orientation, such as Director-general (Charles Farr) head of OSCT, had in my view, confirmed the inevitable and the opportunity to set a new course during this event was inevitable. This was an ideal 'opportunity knocks' situation for frontline service, professionals and organisations. When questioned from those attending the review, on the broader use of expertise outside of their own jurisdiction, it was apparent that their 'orientation' in this sense was off course; and those that had been undermined and that possessed the relevant expertise to bring foreclosure, suggested that a new impetus on selecting appropriate organisation and services to deliver their objectives, needed to be taken more seriously. This was in danger of watering down and neglecting the expertise offered and ran the risk of extremism growth. On this point, they welcomed contributions from frontline practitioners, organisations and professionals with 'open arms'. This process involved all those that were present at the review, firstly, in helping to shape Prevent's future objectives (during a roundtable discussion) and secondly, in helping to distinguish what did and did not work in regards to delivery. Yet, as promising as this was, this did not exclude OSCT from categorising some with good intentions to prevent extremism as 'unfit for the purpose'. Some of these inherited liabilities were due to the previous labours government's lack of funding control, accountability and management.

Given the purpose and nature of the consultation, and in the views of some in attendance, significant failures of the previous Prevent agenda have largely been attributed to bureaucratic weakness in the following categories; *overspending by government, lack of focus, reluctance to support religious and theological discussions, lack of financial accountability and services that lacked the structure, expertise and capacity to deliver*[81]. With a view to discharge themselves of any liability from past Labour failures and to revive the focus under the current government, it was also of importance to distinguish successes. The coalition government would recognise these points in the 2011

---

81   The Prevent Consultation, December 2010, Birmingham.

published review stressing that, *'In future, Prevent will be prioritised according to the risks we face and not (as has been the case) on the basis of demographics'.* Furthermore, *'evaluation and performance monitoring has been weak and they must now be improved. Data collection has been inadequate. It has not always been possible to understand what funding has been used for, or what impacts projects had'*[82].

The Home office under no illusion, sought to monitor and regulate services more closely. This certainly raised a few eyebrows during the review and with the pending decision to finalise preferred organisations to fund in the immediate atmosphere, sent jitters through many organisations that were 'unfit for the purpose'. Given these new measures some withdrew voluntarily. In their final executions, the need to focus on prevention work stood out. This left open the questions of credibility, switching the onus back onto services and agencies to 'come up with the goods'. In light of prevention and in driving this attainment forward, its overall objectives must translate into a tangible set of outcomes that will, as stipulated from our definition earlier *'prevent the thing before it happens'.* On this notion, a report issued by DEMOS, a think-tank on terrorism, highlights the subject of prevention work suggesting and informing us where targeted work should be situated. For example, *'Prevention work should focus on targeted interventions where there is a clear, identified danger or groups or individuals undergoing radicalisation to violence'.* On this point, the revised Prevent agenda has granted access for services to direct their efforts and attention at potential breeding grounds where the risk of recruitment is largely problematic. Other contributions were both warranted and have been dynamic.

As already discussed from the outset, a major response to extremism was demonstrated with ACPO (Association of Chief Police Officers) engagement. The Channel project was a multi-agency approach that sought to make an indelible impression. Set up in 2006, it provided the necessary structure, enabling ongoing support to a variety of organisations delivering counter-terrorism work and to entertain the many referrals that would be forwarded to them for specialist intervention. Their remit would also cover the following, partnership working with local authorities and the wider community. This enclave also complemented key safeguarding publications surrounding issues of assessment, risk and harm. It is here where we can see the Prevent agenda

---

82   Prevent Review 2011 s3.43, 3.44, 3.45.

in reference to delivering objective two, '*Protecting Vulnerable people[83]*' come into clearer focus and where this has an essential linkage to (s)11 of the Children Act 2004 in reference to assessing vulnerable children and young people. This was promising. As discussed from the opening chapter, Professor Monroe speaking on this subject of prevention, states, '*preventative services can do more to reduce abuse and neglect than reactive services.*'[84] It is here where Prevent, in collaboration with social services can help to respond to these vulnerabilities within the wider context of extremism. These formations will enable safeguarding systems and processes to correspond to extremism vulnerabilities more definitively. In this transcendence, the need to educate professionals on preventing violent extremism was significant and was advantageous in a number of ways, For example to alleviate any barriers to the process and to answer any pending questions on this new agenda and for the purpose of partnership working.

TRAINING PROFESSIONALS ON PREVENTING VIOLENT EXTREMISM AND TERRORISM

The need to educate a wide range of professionals was an integral and a critical part of the process. With very few skilled in all sectors to accommodate this demand, it required receptivity from others, especially from the Home Office. The events of July 7th launched another promising venture, allowing many to deliver multiple training programmes across the UK (and in my view randomly) to educate many professionals, given that the terrifying prospect of another 7/7 lingered. For example, the collaboration between organisations such as YJB (Youth Justice Board) and OSCT (Office of Security and Counter-Terrorism) initially helped dictate the process by delivering 'scripted training programmes' across the UK. These have included the Home Office, WRAP – Workshop to Raise Awareness of Prevent (WRAP 2) and PVE – 'Preventing Violent Extremism' in drastic efforts to transmogrify and mobilise professionals. Significant problem arose within this process.

For example, professionals employed in sectors such as education, social work, youth offending and CAMHS (Child and Adolescent Mental Health Services) have struggled to grasp the complexities surrounding topics such as Islam and terrorism, not to forget the profound nature to their historical origins. For those who attended the training, the obscure, or for some contentious, aspects of these sessions related to these and other subjects required

---

83   HM Government – Prevent Strategy 2011 (page 55 objective two: protecting vulnerable people).

84   The Monroe Review, 2011.

drastic consolidation. For example, understanding the confrontations and interaction between the variations of Islamic groups, understanding the reasons behind these confrontations due to these variation of Islamic groups that have formed, was a mere 'tip of the iceberg' Diachronically, it was becoming more obvious these scripted training programmes were unable to answer the burning question surrounding the complex nature revolving around safeguarding children in terms of identifying distinct trends, signs and symptoms. Yet, I postulate, with all unfolding events centred on extremism at the moment, this is still very much underdeveloped in social research. Those less optimistic and unimpressed about these training programmes encouraged some to explore alternatives in an effort to fulfil such voids.

To aggravate matters further, the distinct use of terminologies associated with terrorism and on subjects such as Islam amongst professionals, was at the best, counter-intuitive stagnating their professional development. For example, the constant use of terms such as 'whabbism', 'Jahiliyah', 'tawheed' or 'radicalisation' has only added to this migraine. This deported some back to 'square one'. Anxieties arose, sentencing many to a mental solitary confinement. It did not stop here. Master classes were developed to explore in more depth and detail aspects pertaining to; the history of Islam, extreme groups and their associations, radicalisation theories, the history of terrorism and international dimensions. Initially, designed for the more advanced professionals, these classes were facilitated with combined expertise from selected organisations with extensive experience, one being the Recora Institute.

As part of this package, a joint residential funded programme initiated between organisations such as OSCT (Office of Security and Counter-Terrorism) and DCSF (now DfE) certainly provided the ideal surrounding in which to discuss matter away from the demands of work. Of course, this generated a high volume of interest from prospective candidates from all over the UK making the task of the selection process even more challenging. When I was selected for such a programme, it was an eye opener and quenched some of the thirst, particularly toward understanding the dynamics of history and the connection of terrorism to religion and vice versa. It is in these instances that we can establish clear processes that have driven forward safeguarding agendas to present themselves within extremism environments. This accelarated the process by encouraging joint efforts to safeguard children and young people, especially in terms of assessing vulnerabilities thereby disrupting recruitment. On this point, it brings us to discuss how social work has and other disciplines have advanced on this agenda.

Their encounter on this explosive agenda, which we have already discussed from the outset, has espoused many social work professionals to new observations and because of these observations, in this sense, has further opened 'new perspectives' arising from these observations. These observations gave credence for professionals to embrace a catalogue of new learnings, which contributed to sharpening their skills, knowledge and enlarging their coasts in the process. These social work transformations have been repeatedly expounded upon within social work research. One of its advocates Professor Jonathan Parker from Bournemouth University has shed some light on this important issue. He explains these point in terms of the 'adaptations' and the 'cultural competences' of social workers to adjust to these new environments, is an 'ever growing phenomenon' On this point, social workers' engagement and contribution on this agenda, though ongoing, is evidence of this advancement. This point has also been raised in the published work of Surinder Guru 'Social work and the War on Terror'. For these and other reasons set forth, the Social Work Taskforce (SWTF) was a government initiative set up in 2008 to explore critical issues in social work advancement. In brief, this required the taskforce to steer the profession towards a preferred direction, in an ever-changing and demanding social environment. The aforementioned points have already received international recognition.

At a conference in San Francisco entitled 'The new international agendas: what role for social work?', Professor Jim Life certainly stamped his approval to embrace the global issues and encouraged others on the need to embrace the wider context of social work and terrorism. He emphasises that, *'in the 21st century, however, while those older issues remain critical, new agendas have emerged, which now dominate the headlines and government', the most significant of these being terrorism and global warming'.* He continues, *'So what does this mean for social work, and for social workers? I believe social work has responses to make, at different levels. One of these, which in the current climate is particularly courageous, is to apply a classical social work systemic analysis to terrorism, refusing simply to pathologise the individual, though of course strongly and unreservedly condemning their violent actions, but seeking to understand those actions in a wider context, just as a social worker would do with any offender. That context is historical, political and cultural, and the actions of terrorists must be understood this way*[85]. These transitions have begun to resonate.

Some social work professionals have already started to acquaint themselves making adjustment where necessary to these transitions. A senior social

---

85   The new international agendas: what role for social work?' San Francisco, USA, 2007

worker at Avon and Wiltshire Mental Health Partnership Trust, has described some of the work the trust's social workers and health colleagues are doing to prevent vulnerable people being radicalised by extremist groups, having delivered preventative work on those at risk of extremism, she admits that tackling extremism isn't the most obvious fit for social workers, '*If you'd told me, when I was signing up to my social work training, that this would eventually be part of my remit, I'd have looked at you with disbelief.*' She adds, '*But a training video that featured the mother of Andrew Ibrahim, a Bristol man jailed for terrorist offences in 2009 (referred to in chapter 1) brought home the need for preventative work in this area.*' She continues, '*If we see being radicalised as a form of psychological abuse, it does fit neatly within safeguarding,*' she says. '*It gives us a good framework for getting all potentially relevant agencies round the table to see what we can bring to it to help and support that person with a view to protecting them from further exploitation and harm.*' Her views have certainly provided the platform for further discussions between professionals and agencies that were susceptible towards embracing this agenda. Given the current safeguarding concerns discussed in chapter one, further mechanisms were put into place to ensure continuity, consistency and compliance. The fact that developing partnerships were and are still in the making and process, made this venture even more promising, this continues to generate a sense of expectation. These partnerships are discussed in more detail in chapter five. However, not everyone is enthusiastic about these formations. An article in the community care magazine in January 2015 has raised the concerns of the problems faced by social workers embracing counter-terrorism work. A Home office consultation guidance on Prevent has sparked considerable dialogue. The guidance states, '*the duty is likely to be relevant to fulfilling safeguarding responsibilities in that local authorities should ensure that there are clear and robust safeguarding policies to identify children at risk*'. Amongst their many duties, these proposals are set to place additional work on social workers to identify extremism. In response to these proposals and guidance, Nushra Mansuri a professional officer of BASW (British Association of Social Workers) stressed in no uncertain terms that, '*how much would this change the role of many professionals including social workers*[86] questioning further that, '*will social workers become another strand of the home office apparatus?*' It is envisaged that this would also see foreseeable changes to publications such as 'working together to safeguard children' to help accommodate these proposals. This has been further exacerbated with the introduction of additional terrorism

---

86 Community Care magazine, January 2015.

legislation, the Counter-terrorism and Security Act 2015. This will place a legal duty on many professionals to respond to the issues of radicalisation and to put into place policies, which will also see TPIM – Terrorism Prevention Investigation Matter, strengthen some of the content introduced by Labour in the form of control orders to relocate terror suspects around the UK. Whilst addressing Royal United Services Institute (Rusi) in London, The Home secretary Theresa May was adamant the legislation was vital. She stressed, that *"This legislation is important, the substance is right, the time is right and the way in which it has been developed is right,"* she continues *"It is not a knee-jerk response to a sudden perceived threat. It is a properly-considered, thought-through set of proposals that will help to keep us safe at a time of very significant danger we are engaged in a struggle that is fought on many fronts and in many forms. It is a struggle that will go on for many years and the threat we face right now is perhaps greater than it ever has been - we must have the powers we need to defend ourselves."*[87] The previous Deputy Prime Minister, Nick Clegg has also endorsed these views, stating, *"When you have a new threat you have to consider, sensibly, led by the evidence, whether the new threat requires a new response"* and according to the Assistant Commissioner Mark Rowley said 'the step-change in the extremist threat will continue even if the violence in Syria and Iraq subsides'. The changes had been backed by an independent review said Clegg and its recommended safeguards incorporated.

In backtracking slightly, to incorporate other imperatives, the training session certainly managed to influence social work input towards engaging on the pending and forthcoming challenges of Prevent work. One of the most burning questions that was brought into light was to do with the issues of vulnerabilities. This was promising. What was highly significant, however, was that this drew particular attention to the notion of 'abuse' as an unexplored phenomenon that would 'fit the vulnerability criteria'. This notion, already entrenched in the minds of professionals from social work backgrounds, has gradually surfaced, with the legitimacy of the problem beginning to take root. This was encouraging, especially in terms of raising the profile. As discussed from the outset, one interesting advocate who has raised these concerns, would be the Lord Mayor of London, Boris Johnson. On elaborating on this issue, he emphasised in no uncertain terms that, *''Radicalisation is a form of child abuse and the authorities must have more power to intervene'.* He continued, *'There is built in the British system a reluctance to be judgemental about some else's*

87   http://www.dailymail.co.uk/wires/pa/article-2846735/New-anti-terror-measures-unveiled.html#ixzz3YKSHjBrH

culture even if that reluctance places children at risk'. In concluding, he said, '*We are familiar by now with the threat posed by the preachers of hate, the extremist clerics who can sow seeds of medicine in the minds of impressionable young people'* This requires strong protest and immediate attention by those responsible.

PREVENT AND SAFEGUARDING - A DEVELOPING PARTNERSHIP

The need for governments to support and contribute to this process for the purpose of establishing and sustaining long-term relationships was critical. This has been clearly demonstrated since 2005. The explicit interactions from the Home Office were designed with the intention to advocate by strengthening communication between themselves and other organisations that were active in countering extremism. In this sense, RICU (Research, Information and Communications Unit based within the Home Office) established in 2007, assisted with providing less complex information by simplifying terminologies in a more user-friendly manner (given that the language used in counter-terrorism agendas, manuals and publications were initially intoxicated with strong intellectual connotations and ambiguities some beyond the comprehension of professionals) inclusive of all professionals involved. Amongst its many functions, RICU collated evidence from a wide range of services delivering Prevent work and also informed those organisations delivering prevention work of the forthcoming development on these agendas as they arose from the Home Office. Circulating this information in the form of newsletters, to those services delivering preventative work, particularly to those working with children and young people, provided an ideal opportunity to showcase their good practice to others. This was less descriptive having a practical appeal, which was displayed in a tangible form. Because of this, it had numerous advantages. The creativity and vision of professionals delivering prevention work was let loose in these publications.

Given these imperatives, community relations strengthened. The informative function of RICU, attempted to mitigate speculation in the process that Prevent was simply about 'spying on communities'. These regular interactions also provided the ideal environment to establish trust between law enforcement agencies and community organisations. Publications would provide the ideal platform to encourage and promote effective dialogue and co-operation and for those sceptics, it was certainly difficult to suggest Home office or security services could manipulate or exaggerate its content. In this sense, Rupert Dore, Head of Community and Partnership Engagement, ACPO Prevent delivery unit, ensured its vision and legitimacy remained core to its original intention. For example, in its first newsletter in 2010 '*Prevent*

Community Engagement Activity a focus on youth' gave the scope that influenced a series of positive publications. Distributed in August 2010 (issue no 001) with an audience that initially comprised of police colleagues and community organisations, it set the stage for greater exposure. This publication attracted numerous community responses. In addition to this, it was also envisaged this would raise the profile of Prevent by informing others about good practice on this agenda and which further attempted to eliminate stigmas in the process that suggested that it was another naïve conception aimed at intelligence gathering. Again, it also reminded us that about our safeguarding duties, in that Rupert Dore continues to stress, *'we all have a duty of care to protect young people and the most vulnerable members of our society from harm, be it in relation to violent extremism, drugs, gangs, knife or gun crime. Therefore the Prevent agenda should be seen no differently to safeguarding against any form of vulnerability'.* Points that were embedded into ACPO's children and young people strategy 2010-2013. One of its priorities was focused on the need to implement early intervention for the purpose of protecting children and young people from harm. This was supported and encouraged through collaboration from a range of services, points that are expounded upon in chapter five.

The aforementioned developments have become one of the vehicles by which counter-terrorism work has been transported across a wide range of services and organisations working with children and young people, encouraging others to come on board and subscribe to this illustrious growth. Of course, incorporated into these newsletters, would be the obvious themes surrounding the safeguarding of children and young people from extremism. A point well documented by ACC Paul Netherton, ACPO lead for Prevent within the children and young people business area, when he stresses, *'The police must work together with young people, and those agencies that engage with young people, to safeguard them and ensure they are being protected from being drawn into situations that could cause them harm'.* As we can now see, the shared attitudes and view pertaining to safeguarding children from extremism would now find its popularity and status alongside counter-terrorism publications capable of existing for many years to come, with an ability to alter its course but not its overall destination. The threats that extremism activity presents, have allowed the current safeguarding concerns from these threats to be addressed through existing counter-terrorism policies, strategies and interventions and in this sense, a true 'network dynamic has evolved.

In fact, the results of the interaction between Prevent and safeguarding have clearly driven forward new publications in these realms, which were explicitly designed for the purpose of 'alternative actions'. For example, a document disseminated by ACPO, entitled *Prevent and safeguarding supporting individuals vulnerable to violent extremism,*[88] was another development in this venture, largely applicable to all those with responsibility for safeguarding children and young people. A critical component of this designation would be visible with a Prevent multi-agency panel's ability to take the lead responsibility on referrals. Again, reiterating the current Prevent strategy position in this matter, emphasising that '*protecting children from harm and promoting their welfare depends on shared responsibility and joint working between different agencies' (Home Office 16:23)*[89]. The compliance and commitment between and from organisations was a critical juncture in this process and given the expertise of LSCB (Local Safeguarding Children Board) in respect to the Children Act 2004 section (2) 11 provided the necessary template for those to assess these risk and threats in accordance to its purpose, which is to '*safeguarding and promoting the welfare of children who may be particularly vulnerable*'[90]. The guidance proved useful.

This guidance informed many on a range of vulnerabilities that were clearly defined as potential opening for recruitment and drivers towards radicalising children and young people. These included; '*children living away from home, migrant children, children who go missing, race and racism, abuse by children and young people and children whose behaviour indicate a lack of behaviour control*'[91]. Given this broad criteria, the responsibility of ownership still needed to be established. In responding, the Channel document emphasised, '*ownership of the risk lies with 'multi-agency channel panel' this is the risk to the individual as a result of their vulnerability*'. In the same vein, it would refer to point 3.3 of its document, that stressed Channel is '*about early intervention to protect and divert people away from the risk they may face before illegality relating to terrorism occurs*'[92]. In all this, the inter-connectedness of these two agendas had combined their expertise to develop a matrix of responses. In recognition of these and Channel interactions, the Deputy Chief Constable Craig Denholm, the ACPO lead on Channel, stated that, '*Channel supports people*

---

88 Prevent and Safeguarding Guidance – 'Supporting vulnerable individuals to violent extremism'.

89 HM Prevent Strategy 2011 (Home Office).

90 Children Act 2004 s11.

91 National Safeguarding Document 2010.

92 Channel Document 2010.

who are vulnerable to being radicalised and drawn into terrorism'. Furthermore, it works in a similar way to other safeguarding, partnership activity where agencies come together to support vulnerable individuals; for example work to address drugs, guns and gang issues through early intervention'.[93] As a result these safeguarding developments, a clear set of targets were proposed and assumed their positions, initially in draft form. These comprised with some of the following;

Action 1, in terms of administrative processes: *We recommend that the existing policies and guidance should be adopted to take account of the risks of radicalisation to violent extremism as identified in chapter 11 of "working to safeguard Children' (2010)*

Action 8, which refers to development;

The local safeguarding children board and the area partnership board for Prevent should plan how to develop the understanding and skills of staff to respond to radicalisation within safeguarding processes. It is recommended that this should be approached by extending the expertise and understanding of safeguarding co-ordinators and other key staff, identifying where additional specialist knowledge is required (e.g. Al Qaeda-inspired narratives). Further guidance is provided...on appropriate and proportionate responses and interventions grounded in universal provision

Its emphasis on action 9 of the proposed documentation, in terms of communication, stressed, *'It is important that all local Safeguarding Children Boards should establish and communicate agreed processes and criteria for safeguarding individuals vulnerable to radicalisation and children who may be at risk through living with or being in direct contact with known extremists.*

Again reminding us of our analysis given in chapter one and on point 14 of these proposals in reference to intervention,

'Early identification of concerns should result in responses being made through Universal provision or through targeted interventions that are 'Appropriate, proportionate responses and interventions'[94].

This proposed development was promising. In Addition, the need to formulate an appropriate and suitable model of assessment, to assist, was essential for encouraging referrals. This was also provided by ACPO. This model was flavoured with criteria that provided the scope and flexible in accommodating a range of factors which enabled many to intervene at the earliest opportunity.

---

93   Channel Document 2010.

94   Ibid.

This relationship had some long-term benefits. This was accessible to most services, especially those working on Prevent. Its main selling point was strengthened by its ability to incorporate a wide range of services working with children and young people, ranging from those with universal needs to more complex and specialist needs, housed in a system of response similar to that of the DoH 'Assessment Framework Model', discussed in chapter one. Its main remit would cover the following; '*Universal provisions, Targeted work with those at risk and Specialist interventions with young people already engaged in or linked to extreme violence*'[95]. In addition, it provided a flow chart that explained the procedures to follow for referrals (similar to those seen with s47 inquiries and in the DoH manual 2000). These consisted of, '*identifying concerns, initial response, multi-agency assessment, delivery of support and review*'[96]. Other guidances were equally as highly significant in their proliferations and sought to secure all routes towards safeguarding children and young people.

The National Safeguarding Delivery Unit Guidance document entitled, '*working together to safeguard children 2010*' reminded local authorities and others of their statutory roles, duties and responsibilities in regards to safeguarding children and young people from harm. In light of this and the aforementioned publications discussed in the opening chapters, Prevent would adopt its recommendations, making the necessary adjustments where required. These promising measures were conflated. This culminated in publications such '*Prevent and safeguarding protocol*'. Prevent, inspired by safeguarding publications and further supported with the various legal apparatus, were the streams that have brought about significant changes in these new realms, a point referred to by a senior official. Sir Norman Beth, Channel project senior officer, in the vanguard of Britain's new anti-terrors laws, suggested that 200 school children as young as three years old are potentially being at risk of harbouring religious extremist views in the future. On this point, he stresses, '*with the help of these communities we can identify the kids, who are vulnerable to the message and influenced by the message. The challenge is to intervene and other guidance, not necessarily to prosecute - as seen with national Prevent working document in 2010 - but to address their grievances, their growing sense of hate and potential to do something violent in the name*

---

95   Prevent and Safeguarding Guidance, supporting individuals vulnerable to violent extremism.

96   Prevent and Safeguarding Guidance, supporting individuals vulnerable to violent extremism, page 10.

of some misinterpretations of faith. [97]' These openings have enabled a range of resources, systems and procedures to cross over into counter-terrorism work. These distinctions were important and were in danger of being misunderstood. Nonetheless, they provided the ideal environment for social work and care professionals to embrace these changes, with fewer complexities began to launch many towards a pathway of counter extremism more comfortably within a social care context. Troubling signs emerged. This was set to become more exhaustive, at least in terms of the potential of the rise of caseloads. I must stress that this is a constant work in progress and could not be left in a state of uncertainty. There were also risks and temptations ahead.

In seeking to find more suspects, particularly those from social sectors, Prevent has tempted social care professionals to become the 'eyes' and 'ears' of the intelligence service. Again, this is in danger of reinforcing speculation pertaining to the suspicions of government-led initiatives accused of 'spying'. This new style of 'human surveillance' sought to tarnish relationships and ran the risk of regression, reinforcing criticisms pertaining to Prevent's legitimacy as an balanced counter-terrorism response, which from its inception, many critics have argued, it was a 'camouflage' for security services which has been termed by some as 'Pursue in sheep's clothing'. These deceptions have left an indelible stain not just on the consciousness of local communities but also on impressionable minds of young people, which cannot be so easily neutralised. More pointedly, many professionals have argued (myself included) that the legal entitlement that grants young people the legitimate right and privilege to express their extreme views, has been tampered with by Prevent. Again, this also presents challenges. It is precisely because of these constraints that could restrict the liberty of young people. This is where I endorse aspects of Professor Kundai's aforementioned report in particular reference to these constraints and restrictions. I have defined this, in term of granting liberty as 'appropriate vocalisation'. This point is apparent in that Professor Kundani stresses that, *'extremism represents a new category of speech'*[98] In this sense, it is loaded with wider implications and requires clarification. This is where I argue that extremism speeches, that do not advocate violence or the use of violence, *'must be provided with some leverage, legal defence and a platform in order to survive'* What is also important to remember here, however, given the fact that being

---

97   The Yemen Post 2010.

98   A Decade Lost, rethinking radicalisation and extremism' Professor Aruni Kundai, Claystones.

British is of significance according to Prevent agenda definition, and is not confined by reason of race, religion or ethnicity in this context, is of considerable importance to countering violent extremism, especially those that are fuelled due to these very reasons that promote these values exclusively to being white or for the purpose of promoting discrimination and dividing communities on this basis. For those extremist, radicals or terrorists, who may suggest, interpret or imply that being British means you must be of 'white heritage' cannot be justified, in this context or in prevents definition. In this sense, those who continue or intend to use violence or extremism against the state on this point, have little or no argument in this context. I must stress whilst on this point, that according to theological views held by many, there is on one race that God recognises and that is the 'human race'. This will help to break down existing barriers, thereby promoting equality and attempt to eliminate discrimination in the process. In saying this, this brings us back to our discussions earlier, Prevent's view of an extremist is one that is 'against British values' and is not against 'freedom of expression'. The preservation of these extreme views, whether distributed by young people or not, will arguably, encourage engagement and provide the scope to promote democracy, without any infringement or violation of human rights. This will generate confidence and help to restore trust from the general public, not just between communities but also towards governments during these processes. Extremism therefore, must have some boundaries, restrictions and regulation. On the point of preservation we must turn to our legal guardians for some validation of these and other points.

According to the CPS (Crown Prosecution Service) the definition of violent extremism must incorporate key strands, which must vividly demonstrate unacceptable behaviour by any medium in expressing these views:

Foment, justify or glorify terrorist violence in furtherance of particular beliefs;

Seek to provoke others to terrorist attacks

Foment other serious criminal activity or seek to provoke others to serious criminal acts; or

Foster hatred which might lead to inter-community violence in the UK[99]

The CPS have emphasised that these could arise through, '*spoken words, creations of tapes and videos of speeches, internet entries, chanting, banners and written notes and publications*'[100]. More importantly, when prosecuting, the

---

99 http://www.cps.gov.uk/publications/prosecutions/violent_extremism.
100 Ibid.

CPS have stressed, according to their website, that courts must bear in mind that people have a right to free speech, which will possess aspects that will also have the 'right to offend'. It is also worth noting, that the courts have ruled that any behaviour that is merely annoying, rude or offensive does not necessarily constitute a criminal offence. In taking these points on board, we must consider some of the problems faced particularly by young people who are discriminated against on these legitimate grounds, or where no concerns to their welfare or safeguarding are in question as some may interpret. These can also been taken out of context by professionals and can deprive young people from basic provisions and entitlements especially for those of British born origin. This is also in danger of reinforcing stereotypes and inviting discrimination. It is here that we must apply some logical application to our hypothesis.

Firstly, the problem of labelling young people inappropriately with views that are observed as 'extreme' without the presence of any violence or threat of use of violence, is according to article 14 of the UN Convention of the Right of the Child, a direct attack on their *freedom of thought or expression*, which according to Article 4 stipulates that *governments shall take all necessary steps to make these rights available to all children*, which in this sense and in practice, is at risk of contradicting itself and appears to have subjected them to regular monitoring by intelligence and security agencies, arguing that democracy, to some extent, is both biased and controlled. This is another point that has been raised as a concern from Ms Manusri from BASW, She stress that, *'my concern is that these proposals give rise to social workers and others being drawn into a very different agenda of surveillance and intelligence gathering for the purposes of countering terrorism which would completely distort their role'*[101]. In this sense, social workers are trained to safeguard and not trained to monitor or gather intelligence, let alone become legal experts in any counter-terrorism sense. Secondly, this may affect the child's or the young person's long-term socio-educational opportunities, given the fact that labels are hard to remove (borrowing from criminological theories on 'labelling effects' come to mind) this can also affect their self-image. Because of these labels, many will find difficulties in obtaining employment or getting into places of further education. And thirdly, these young people may rebel against the 'system' and thus the policy becomes counterproductive to the UK campaign against extremism, steering many young people towards perusing alternatives because of these negative experiences.

---

101 Community Care magazine, January 2015.

This is disturbing and will grant more sentiment towards extremism. I must inform readers, particularly those working with children and young people, that gaining the trust of any groups is a vital ingredient towards securing and developing relationships to prevent problems. Having worked extensively with young people over the years has convinced me that trust is a key component of granting access and towards promoting change. Whilst on this point, research has suggested, that *'trusting relationships are an inevitable consequence of meaningful experience'.* Furthermore, it was the DfE that has emphatically stressed that, *'a key part of effective communication and engagement is trust, both between the workforce, children, young people and their carers, and between and within different sectors of the workforce itself'*[102] *(DfES, 2003, page 6).* Again, Prevent was at risk of damaging these relationships.

With the best of government intentions, reluctance from young people to engage or attend voluntary programmes such as Prevent or even other related intervention programmes for that matter, have become a regular occurrence. More crucially, these apprehensions and anxieties have been reflected in local communities who have become sceptical of any initiatives aimed at tackling extremism or terrorism, even in the vetted interest of promoting public safety, particularly those dictated by governments. This also led to fears that government intended to impose sanctions. It terms of my experience, having observed these anxieties and tension first hand during group delivery, the clear reluctance of young people to open up and share, has been problematic at times, uncomfortable and counter-productive especially within the context of this agenda and in terms of promoting socialisation, cohesion and for reconciliation purposes. These interactions have resulted in highly charged emotional confrontations (even within a controlled and fostered environment) between professionals and amongst young people stemming from the challenges of exploring profound and controversial subjects such as, terrorism, British values, Islam, religion and racism, to name a few. I must stress here, having been one of Prevent's committed disciples early on, that Prevent was somewhat ambitious in its attempts to counter violent extremism, having initially lacked the insight to project the unforeseen problems and risks in practice. In spite of this, the credibility of Prevent has continued to establish itself.

Organisationally then, post 7/7 there has commenced a revolution involving statutory, voluntary, private, charitable and other sectors, and

---

102 Department for Education and Skills, 2003.

those attempting to enlarge their coasts to incorporate wider imperatives of counter-terrorism work. To help accommodate this, the Prevent agenda carried with it the idea and notion of work based Prevent co-ordinators and leads. Their purpose, institutionally, to respond and serve on a range matters pertaining to violent extremism and terrorism. In closing this chapter, it has swiftly become evident that traces of Prevent's success as safeguarding respondent are now largely recognised. According to the Home Office, *'Local authorities are increasingly recognising Prevent as an important issue in safeguarding young people. According to a DfE assessment in March 2010, 61% of local authorities' children's services were actively engaged in Prevent work and had a specific plan in place to engage schools (though this does not necessarily reflect on whether the quality and scope of that engagement is appropriate). This is an increase of 11% from 2009'* (Home Office)[103]. These statistics were the evidence that informed us that services have begun to reciprocate towards Prevent.

---

103 Department for Education, 2010.

5: Working Towards an Inter-Agency Response

'Effective information sharing is key to the delivery of Prevent'.

Another paradigm shift occurred due to the terrorist attacks in 2005, this time involving services. Attention was paid to the role that agencies could play in preventing extremism and those, not yet involved, but that had the heightened interest to incorporate partnership working on counter-terrorism agendas as part of their extended remit, were welcomed on board. One of the criteria that was imposed, was primarily centred on establishing internal infrastructures, systems and processes that would accommodate the wider imperatives of counter-terrorism work and was one of considerable importance towards influencing the orientation of inter-agency working on this new agenda. Because of extremist sophistications, services were also required to adapt and design unique responses, which in hindsight, were also influenced against the backdrop of bureaucratic banter surrounding extremist semantics, which could not be dialectically defined by political figures or security experts alone. This required 'all hands on deck' from services that were committed to safeguarding people from extremism. Formations began and templates emerged. For example, most LAs (Local Authorities) now display covert messages informing all those concerned about any suspicious actions or behaviours of individuals that might have the traits of violent extremism or terrorism, on their council website, advising on the procedures to follow, in terms of reporting these concerns. These have been referred to as 'Safeguarding and Extremism' offering a discreet and confidential service for members of the public. Within these formations, OSCT provisions were utilised with precision.

Officers from special divisions such as CTU (counter-Terrorism Unit) were mobilised to assist with local councils' concerns, given the council constraints, lack of expertise and boundaries, especially where matters required serious investigation or the security of the state was threatened. It was becoming abundantly clear that the Home Office had graduated to another dimension, especially within counter-terrorism realms by acquiring a 'messianic role' due to this agenda. Some of this was demonstrated in their ability to provide and disseminate resources, advice and information to a wide range of services and organisations delivering preventative work and in bringing services together for the purpose of mobilisation, as discussed in the previous chapter This was further strengthened by the Home Office's ability to take the lead and despite the lack of commitment from others, it remained undeterred in its vision by complying to their own stipulations which, according to Prevent, stated that, *'we intend that agencies and departments work to a common set of objectives in this area'*[104]. In one respect, this was quite obvious given the reasons to engage, in a safeguarding sense, was everyone's statutory responsibility. In fact, numerous pieces of legislation already existed that ensured this continuity and also placed a duty on local authorities and others, towards sharing information amongst themselves in an active and safe manner. It is needful to understand these for the purposes of engagement, compliance and individual and corporate responsibility. In 2008 a HM Government document entitled *Information sharing – guidance for practitioners and managers*, had already set a context, prescribing key principles that should govern the linguistics of sharing information between staff and agencies. Its comprehensive six-point guide for practitioners enabled many to govern their covert affairs more pointedly. The problems of safeguarding that had once remained hidden or invisible would eventually be exposed through the lenses of extremism activity and require these legal impositions to respond.

These aforementioned duties are prescribed in the following. The Local Government Act 1972, section three, provides the local authority, *'power to do anything... Which is calculated and facilitated...'* and the Local Government Act 2000 section 2 (1) provides, *'that every local authority shall have the power to do anything which they consider is likely to achieve the promotion or improvement of the economic, social and well-being of the area'.* In terms of individual and corporate responsibility. These are enshrined in the following. The Data Protection Act 1998, The Human Rights Act 1998, The Common Law Duty of Confidence, The Crime and Disorder Act 1998, The Children Act 2004 Sections 10 and 11. In terms of disclosures of offenders, the Offender Management Act (OMA) 2007 enforces the following in section 14, *'enables disclosures of information to or from providers of probation services, by or to Government departments, local authorities, Youth Justice board, Parole boards, chief officers of police and relevant contractors, where other purposes connected with the management of offenders.'* Other services, such as the Children and Family Court Advisory and Support Service (CAFCASS) also have a duty under section 12(1) of the Criminal Justice and Court Services Act 2000 to

---

104 Prevent agenda 2011 (Objective 3) 7.1.

safeguard and promote the welfare of children involved in family proceedings in which their welfare is, or may be, in question.

Other professionals, with direct responsibility for assessment and treatment of children include clinical and educational psychologists, paediatricians and nurses. Assessment by these professionals may provide significant information, such as observing behavioural changes due to the presence of extreme views that will influence negative or even violent behaviour. This may alert professionals to safeguarding concerns. Moreover, PCTs (Primary Care Trusts) hold key responsibilities when it comes to child welfare, and are under a duty to make arrangements to ensure when discharging their functions, they have regard to safeguarding and promoting the welfare of children when a child is discharged, and must consider their obligations in discharge, given S85 of CA 1989, requiring a PCT to notify responsible authorities where a child's residence is and in this sense, assess vulnerability and risk. Early years providers have a duty under section 40 of the Childcare Act 2006 to comply with the welfare requirements of the Early Years Foundation Stage, under which providers are required to take necessary steps to safeguard and promote the welfare of young children. For those employed in health sectors, section 251 of the NHSA and Section 60 of the HSCA provide a power for the Secretary of State to make regulations governing the processing of patient information, which can't be ignored, even if the staff are concerned that a patient is harbouring extremist views. A joint report published by the Royal College of medicine stated that, 'Clinicians must clearly understand their responsibilities around safeguarding children'. It continues, 'all doctors must be able to recognise children at risk of radicalisation'. According to one organisation, to date an estimated 44,000 healthcare professionals have gone through extremism training already. Those responsible for securing our borders would also have to comply. The UKBA (United Kingdom Border Agency) is required under section 55 of the Borders, Citizenship and Immigration Act 2009 to carry out its existing functions in a way that takes into account the need to safeguard and promote the welfare of children in the UK. Section 55 is intended to have the same effect as section 11 of the Children Act 2004.

In addition to the statutory requirements to share information and to safeguard, extended measures were carefully crafted from these existing laws that were applicable to safeguarding children and young people from extremism. This also drove forward safeguarding legislation in the direction of counter-terrorism agendas and was a driving force for change. This significance has been translated into publications that have continued to shape policies and procedures and refused to be subjected to any laxity due to professional opinions, views or perspectives. The 'hallmark' of government endorsement of the publications, which have been promulgated throughout this material, further informed and warned professionals to be cognizant of their safeguarding responsibilities. These consolidations particularly relevant to safeguarding from extremism are comprised and housed in the following enactments; Children Act 1989 and 2004; Working together to safeguard children (2010); Framework for the assessment of children in need and their families (2000); Channel: Supporting individuals vulnerable to recruitment by violent extremists: A Guide for Local Partnerships, HM Government with Association of Chief Police Officers, 2010; and the revised national CONTEST (Counter-Terrorism Strategy) 2011. The most recent has been seen with the Counter-Terrorism and Security Act 2015 which comes into force 1st July 2015, in that *'to have due regard to the need to prevent people from being drawn into terrorism'*, which places a legal duty on professionals to respond to risks and concerns of radicalisation, reinforcing safeguarding responsibilities as a result. European contributions were furnished through articles and conventions.

The strongest statement of duty to combat terrorism in the case-law of the European Court of Human Rights is to be found in the decisions concerning the positive obligations imposed by the right to life in Article 2 of the Convention, Courts have interpreted Article 2(1) to *'take appropriate steps to safeguard the lives of those within its Jurisdiction'*. Corresponding European directives sought to exercise their authority where matters of safeguarding arose. These legislative thrusts pushed forward the European Conventions, reminding us that protecting children from any harm, violence or the threat of the use of violence required drastic action,

Children have the right to be protected from all forms of violence. They must be kept safe from harm. They must be given proper care by those looking after them (A.19) International Human Rights Standards.

Having applied the statutory and legal requirements to safeguard shortened the proximity that had previously existed between agencies and, with the inclusion of Prevent, were the finishing touches required to close the gap. Moreover, it was inevitable that the dialogue between these agencies on this agenda would compel them towards becoming more interdependent, providing the finishing touches. This transcendence has its origins, and can be traced back over numerous years, deriving primarily from safeguarding cases. One, in particular, was notable in paving the way.

It would be during 1987 that allegations of sexual abuse came to the attention of social services. These concerns were related to children living in Cleveland. An inquiry in 1988 led by Elizabeth Butler-Sloss was a robust response to these concerns. The 'Cleveland report' as it would eventually be coined, was an intrinsic response to analyse the failures of social services to safeguard vulnerable children, many that, astonishingly, were admitted into hospital in their droves due to these concerns. As feared, what was identified as some of the failures that were contributory to this predicament and what was lacking in scope and provision would eventually be employed as recommendations within the final report. The influence of the report gave credence to prescribe major reforms to be implemented in a range of paradigmatic settings, especially where children were integral to the service provided. In brief, the report's findings tied up the loose ends by informing professionals to fall into line by promoting communication, co-operation and dialogue between agencies and not for any one person or organisation to make hasty decisions in isolation, especially where the matter of safeguarding was the determinative factor. These exchanges and failures were most common between police and social services during the 80s, and where it was recognised closer and regular communication between agencies involved in safeguarding and child protection needed to take priority. This was one of the major overhauls that was responsible for the introduction of landmark legislation that would shift the entire safeguarding cargo towards new directions, principally, in the form of 'the Children Act 1989' implemented in 1991, which has already been discussed in chapter one. Since then, numerous consultations, reviews and publications have suggested and recommended ways forward, including DoH (Department of Health) framework assessment 2000, the Children Act 2004, the green paper on Working Together to Safeguard Children 2006 and National Safeguarding Document 2010. However, despite this impressive track record, significant failures and chronic limitations have warranted further governmental intervention. Because of these and other ongoing predicaments, a thorough review of the child protection system in the UK was an aim to go beyond convention. The government, less enthusiastic about the current system's potential, often questioning 'why systems were failing children', sought to make an indelible impression through the medium of ongoing recommendations and independent reviews. To make this point is to reinforce the contention that is necessarily the focus of numerous publications and safeguarding failures and reviews, as discussed from the outset. This may be expected to continue for many years to come.

The Munro Review (led by Professor Eileen Munro) was a robust response to child protection within England. Commissioned by the previous Education Secretary Michael Grove in 2010, the report, *The Munro Review of child protection, 'A child system approach'* was officially published in 2011 for the DfE. Given this unique opportunity, Professor Monroe 'took the bull by the horns' and 'left no stone unturned'. In short, her report identified some of the handicaps that disabled current systems which, syntactically, prevented progress. On reflection of the review, and in reference to those systems that were operating during the time of review, she categorically stressed that there was need for more occupancy, which was a crucial factor for progression in these highly charged social environments and emphasised the need for a *'systems approach framework'* to be more forthcoming. Crucially, these changes would enable a more child-centred approach to flourish in these settings, and one that had less 'bureaucratic and compliance emphasis' which was recognised as stagnating progress. Furthermore she stressed that this system must focus on the 'practicalities' of safeguarding the welfare of children and young people. This was taken further with Professor Munro's preference for a *'socio-technical approach'*[105] to become more transparent and was one that would promote positive synergies between the organisations and their staff. Her summary of recommendations - though numerous - with particular emphasis on point 2 of her report was implicit and highly decorated, suggesting that *'the inspection framework should exercise the effectiveness of the contribution of all local services'*[106] For the purpose of this chapter and its relevance towards applying appropriate systems in children's services and for the safeguarding of children and young people, especially now from extremism, this has valuable currency. We must also account for human error that is the culprit responsible for failures that affect, jeopardise and disable these systems. Because of these errors, we must not forget, that quite often, safeguarding discourse has also been linked with the 'misclassification of judgements' that have derived from the quality of the 'analysis of case notes' of professional errors that have also obstructed the overall elections and decisions to safeguard. A point repeatedly voiced and reiterated by Professor Munro, in that a *'significant number of 'misclassifications' that are apparent with the system, needs to be addressed';* this invokes questions. In brief, her recommendations sought to encourage 'organisational transformations' by encouraging services towards developing internal systems that have a strong emphasis on *'effective management procedures'* particularly

---

105 The Munro Review 2011.

106 Ibid.

pertaining to the myriad number of children and young people that would come through the doors (in our case those involved within extremism) rather than depending on pre-existing systems that were outdated, insufficient and unable to fluctuate, as a strength for inter-agency working. It is here that we can applaud those services, by suggesting that any system that delivered these practical objectives to safeguard, without breaching the confidentiality of the service's users and in the process preserved the professional integrity of its workers, was a 'dream come true'. These criteria echo points raised by those responsible for the regulation of these and related sectors, one being social work. The GSCC Code of Conduct states social workers must:

'Protect the rights and promote the interests of service users and carers; Promote the independence of service users while protecting them as far as possible from danger or harm; and respecting the rights of service users while seeking to ensure that their behaviour does not harm themselves or other people.'

For the reasons set forth, reviews, consultations and publications have become a common trend throughout the years pertaining to the safeguarding of children and young people and due to the terrorist attacks in 2005, have invited parliamentary rhetoric into social care areas, particularly in the form of consultation, questions and debates. In this sense, Home Office consultations on Prevent had already taken these opportunities by removing sanctions and creating widespread dialogue outside of institutional and conventional norms, comprising a target audience from all over the UK. For example, the inclusion of the local religious and cultural communities by the Home Office, seldom seen within social work consultation on safeguarding issues, implies a new impetus had been initiated. These co-ordinated events drove forward governmental motivations by generating interest. However, I must stress that their overall objectives were clear, yet on the other hand, their intent and scope were not as clear. At the other end of the spectrum, when we consider the wider implications of inter-agency strength and sustainability, it also relates to the skills, knowledge and expertise of staff employed as an essential component to the make-up of inter-agency working and progression. The difficulty, and at the same time mistakes with Prevent, in this sense, was to attract suitably trained professionals to implement the aforementioned measures and to identify any one person to facilitate and develop effective systems and take lead responsibility to implement these measures within a wide range of settings and institutions and which was another daunting task in itself. Troubling signs emerged.

Hence, to alleviate anxiety and to avoid any negative repercussions, the task of recruitment was left at the discretion of the funded organisation, to formulate job descriptions, advertise posts, and manage these potential employees. With very little to go off, this seemed a task beyond the service's own management expertise and at best was envisaged as an 'unrealistic prospect' to find appropriate and exceptional candidates, given that everybody was new to this terrorism agenda. Nonetheless this did not stop the campaign. It was and would become obvious, that some candidates who applied lacked some of the basic credentials, especially in terms of possessing the relevant experience or qualifications, let alone proclaiming to have any expertise on extremism or terrorism, and for some it was their first encounter working with children and young people within any social care or professional setting. In spite of this, the 'exotic appeal' of working on terrorism agendas, especially those loaded with prestige and benefits for example 'attending Home Office consultation and reviews' attracted many individuals. Initially, this gave allowance in terms of employment to positively discriminate and due to the terrorist attacks in 2005 influenced by Islamist extremists, the vast amount of candidates that applied and were subsequently employed on counter-terrorism agendas given the vague criteria at the time, were perceived as be given preferential treatment. This was exclusive to those with particular religious pedigree and from cultural backgrounds. This sparked questions that were salient on the minds of many professionals, why?

The employment of those from Muslim backgrounds, for example, was to some extent, a reactionary response, stemming primarily because of the threats of Islamist extremism to the UK, post 7/7. Though this was appreciated in terms of supplying knowledge of subjects such as Islam, Islamic history and the Quran, to counter those Islamist extremists and threats; it has, however, in hindsight, has shown there are weakness and challenges to this in terms of delivery, operations and engagement. For example, the need to gain the relevant knowledge and acquire the skills to deter children and young people from extremism and to develop appropriate interventions requires more than just a working knowledge of or reciting of religious texts - though useful in countering distorted versions of religion – do not totally suffice to fulfil the broader and current task at hand. To put it bluntly and in engagement terms, do white young males with extreme views, some which may be in context with upholding legitimate British values, who are referred to Prevent programmes of intervention, due to these legitimate views that are deemed odious to some and that which have brought direct conflict with Muslims in local communities, find it conducive or even logical, to be assigned a Muslim worker with the intention to conduct in-depth sessions of intervention, knowing the risk to both parties? Can the trust between the young white male and the professional, genuinely, be built in these cases given the barriers that already exist or that may present themselves during the process of engagement? A sharper focus is needed. This will better protect bother parties and help to maintain the relationship. It is also here that I postulate, given the powerful position of Prevent workers, that the danger of exploitation could also arise in these instances. This was apparent with one of the July 7th bombers, whose privileged position as a mentor working with children has already raised some disturbing questions. Similarities have been recognised and drawn during Prevent programmes of evaluation. These points can also have wider implications on the broader context of inter-agency working, which need to be taken seriously in further Prevent deliberations.

For example, in 2010 an evaluation by Newham London Borough Council previously highlighted the use of Imams on Prevent as being counter-productive in some respects. It would be brought to light, that some lacked the credentials to work effectively on these agendas, suggesting a new impetus was needed. As a consequence, the need to educate Imams to upskill their knowledge on a wide range of matters was evident. This ran the risk of repeating itself, but in a wider context. It is here that workers are reminded about the 'power dynamics and structural inequalities' that exist in wider society and where theories of pro-social modelling all have significance to the wider context of Prevent delivery. Some, given the reasons why they initially applied for such demanding posts, have 'bitten off more than they can chew', having not considered the broader implications, in this sense. These weaknesses and voids in practice have also hindered progress. This could prove costly in preventing extremism in the short and long-term.

It is needful and for the purpose of this chapter, that I have referred to some of these disadvantages and hindrances, for examples some of the following: the lack of understanding and defining of British values, difficulties with communication (cultural, and language barriers), inability to critically analyse programmes of intervention (strength and weakness, design, analysis and evaluation) lack of awareness on the theoretical frameworks and models on intellectual, emotional and psychological development of children and young people (Piaget, Erikson, Freud etc) as discussed in the previous chapters. By dissecting these analytically, it will help to raise awareness by contextualising and compartmentalising distinct patterns, trends, perceptions and behaviours that are prevalent and influential during children's and young people's social, emotional, intellectual and psychological development to the advantage of the practitioner knowledge base and for the effective application in delivery, particularly, within a diverse range of settings. This is an important aspect, especially for those professionals working extensively on counter-terrorism agenda.

This information is quite useful, especially for those preparing to engage on counter-terrorism work and for inter-agency advancement. This has its practical and operational advantages. For example, its ability to influence the formal stages of designing and implementing appropriate interventions, for group work engagement and for the purpose of conducting detailed assessments with a view towards engaging in one to one intensive sessions. Whilst on this point, having obtained such skills, knowledge and experience over the years, and by the use of logical application, it has enriched my thinking and helped shaped my professional practice to effectively engage with children and young people more confidently, especially on this and similar agendas. This has enabled me to flourish, especially in terms of preventing extremism, preventing anti-social, criminal and offending behaviour, group and one to one work, conducting detailed assessments and producing effective outcomes, that have promoted the interest and needs of children and young people.

Having realised this, this brings us to the question of the credibility of the Prevent professional to deliver Home Office expectation. Having already discussed this, it begs other questions and at the same time offers suggestions. The recommendation of a balanced taskforce, comprising of all faiths, races and cultures and from a range of professional backgrounds who are capable of delivering these objectives, needs to be taken more seriously if we are to progress. Because of these differences, it was noticeable that these voids have contributed to the hidden tensions within this rapidly developing agenda and organisations that were seeking to accommodate Prevent provisions, were discouraged. At this point, it is uncertain how much of this had driven services to seek alternatives to the Prevent agendas for the reason set forth in chapter four, in light of the Prevent consultation and subsequent reforms.

Unsurprisingly, these deficiencies have given rise to additional contentions between Prevent professionals and colleagues. The various opinions (such as use of intervention and referrals) pertaining to the vulnerabilities of the child and young person's welfare, were at the best of times, splintered, and were certainly suggestive that not everybody was 'singing from the same hymn book' - this sought to damage any vibrant co-existence and relationship that hinged itself on the aforementioned processes, that were contributory to inter-agency survival. Crucially, those delivering extremism interventions can only be appropriately managed where there is a clear 'transparency' between all agencies involved, especially in delivery and which does not seek to overlook where there are ineffective structures, systems and assessments that are inadequate, and that the needs of the child and young person are conclusively agreed, finalised then actioned in accordance with the relevant guidelines, policies and protocols.

The contribution from all sectors involved cannot be ignored or taken as trivial, whether statutory, voluntary, charitable, third or private sectors. These must be given an 'equal platform' to perform, thereby providing what government publications on safeguarding and now Prevent, over the years, have so earnestly desired to protect, and encourage, namely *sharing and joint responsibility*. On the other hand, to avoid any disenchantment between counter-terrorism agendas and wider sectors, it is here, where I postulate, having been involved in similar situations, that during these exchanges and transitions, Prevent professionals can contribute dramatically to these correlative aspects and are also key to binding these processes together. The danger of isolating or undermining professionals with the relevant expertise can weaken inter-agency progress. Our investigations arrive to some conclusion. For example, it is deeply mistaken to say any one assessment or approach is adequate for all services, yet, is only relevant to that service by virtue of exclusivity, suggesting that a singular template (similar to that of CAF) must be considered for Prevent to help encourage service engagement, with a view to simplifying any technicalities during this process. Reminding us that, 'poor quality assessments' or 'interventions' by professionals could weaken service engagement and allow 'extremists' to slip through the net and in this case, there are no 'exceptions to the rule' as far as governments and security services are concerned. Those who are reading this material may well want to exercise some cautious optimism, before jumping into this highly demanding agenda.

Continuing on the notion of partnership working, the impact of the July 7th terrorist attacks was another 'trigger point' and opportunity to evaluate. For example, in 2009 the Home Office and the DCSF (now DfE) commissioned research on extremism, in collaboration with the Office for Public Management (OPM), an independent public researcher, and the National Foundation for Educational Research (NFER), the UK's largest provider of research, assessment and information services for education, training and children's services. The report entitled *Teaching approaches that help to build resilience to extremism among young people*[107] was one of considerable importance, informing us of effective ways to build resilience against extremism. The report critically explored the teaching methods, knowledge, skills and behaviours that help to build resilience. The research was conducted with an in depth analysis of 10 case studies of relevant projects, primarily from an educational perspective. It reinforced the notion of inter-agency working as a key component to this success.

This information was informative and proved beneficial towards encouraging partnership working and in this sense, offered some scope. In its final publication, it unreservedly referred to what our central theme in this chapter, has alluded to, chiefly, *'effective partnership working with local* agencies', encouraging further, all sectors towards, *'ways to ensure that interventions' potential impact can be maximised'*[108]. This can only be achieved through applying the fundamental principles that under-pin and support effective partnership working. Some of these have been identified as, *'open communication between agencies, which helps to generate shared understanding about the aims, methods and expected outcomes of the interventions (for the long-term) regular feedback on impact achieved'.* This then leads us towards the logical application of these principles in practice.

THE NEED TO COLLABORATE

As we have been discussing, contributions to inter-agency working were necessary and, moving on to look at another point, current research has suggested that services delivering preventative work should work within 'their remit' keeping aspects distinct and encouraging very little overlap where possible. This has also been identified as an integral part of effective change. For example, security services that hold key responsibility to ensure the safety of the British public, positioned at all levels, must allow grassroots organisations to deliver programmes of intervention without the urgency or tendency to monitor and interfere in these progresses, especially in environments where social cohesion or the integration of communities presents little chance of finding any 'suspects' (given the view held by those young people from these communities may seem extreme, but are not dangerous). On the other hand, any disclosures or evidence ascertained from these settings, that were highly suggestive that the terrifying prospect of a terrorist threat, association or attack could materialise, would immediately reverse this notion, and the need

---

107 'Teaching approaches that help to build resilience to extremism among young people' DfE 2010 (DfE-RR119).

108 Ibid.

to inform police or the security service would certainly became operative. However, given the former view, the interference of government, security or intelligence services, has also hindered progress and sparked jitters amongst organisations delivering counter-terrorism work. Nonetheless, despite these interferences, the prevailing concerns, especially where the danger of extremism or terrorism growth has threatened safety, have taken precedence. This has wider implications in practice.

In applying this point, social workers and other professionals are there-fore subject to conform to these preventative measures to assess children and young people whose problematic behaviour fall within this context of 'extreme' almost on a daily basis, some that are taking the motionless form of *observational risk assessment*. In not drifting away from the main selling point, this ensured that the welfare of children was maintained was core in these observations and undoubtedly, kept the safeguarding wheel turning. This drove forward increased dialogue. These dialogues took the form of boardroom discussions with heads of services addressing common themes, risks and concerns of extremism. By cascading these concerns to departments - and given the role of frontline professionals here, we are already reminded about the severity of harm to which children and young people were exposed - in this sense, the need to collaborate was accelerated. Beyond the practi-calities of counter-terrorism officer presence in these matters, the impor-tance of inter-agency working has conceptually, been ratified with numerous landmark reviews that have already been 'set in stone' reminding us of our commitment to collaborate. Professionally speaking, our central theme is not just about protecting or safeguarding an object or thing but, according to my theological view, 'life itself'. Children and young people in this sense, as put in the words of Lord Justice Baroness Butler-Sloss, are of equal standing, *'the child is a person not an object of concern'.*[109] On this point, we look at some of the challenges to this task.

CHALLENGES TO INTER-AGENCY WORKING

In terms of change, I think that we can all agree that any form of change can often give rise to resistance.

This presents internal challenges that are also applicable in our professional practice. These resistances have been responsible for creating barriers and have also hindered the progress of effective partnership working. This has given rise to a range of problems, some that I postulate, have also been 'self-inflicted'.

---

109 The Munro Review, 2011.

Some of these problems have been visible from a range of interactions that have involved tensions related to *'dispositional disputes'* and *'domain disputes'*. These have their origins, some emanating from problems that some have observed as *'conflicts that may occur where there is a degree of overlap of responsibility between two agencies with a consequent blurring of boundaries[110]'*. This blurring of boundaries can also create alienation, which for the purpose of advancing inter-agency working, can be frustrating.

It is here that Prevent workers are also at risk of contributing to these dynamics. These may exist due to questions arising from a range of observations that are undermined or even overlooked as insignificant, for example *'value of exchange of information', 'confidentiality and variations of professional judgement'.* I will elaborate on a couple of these with examples that will serve to demonstrate these points. The *'value of exchange of information'* on counter-terrorism agendas has been identified as one barrier, which has already been discussed in the previous chapter. The Home Office response saw RICU provide some respite through publications. Others are demonstrated between professionals in contradistinction to the *'variations of professional judgement'* pertaining to prospective referrals, some that have been ambiguous, ambitious and at times, discursive. This could also affect external referrals to channel and run the risk of allowing potential extremist to slip through the net. These points have implication in practice.

For example, what social workers or teachers may observe as an angry Pakistani child with hostility towards British soldiers in foreign countries having watched Al Jazeera, which could quite easily be ignored or perceived as a sudden mood swing or moment of anger, which on the other hand may be interpreted by those working on the preventing extremism agenda, as incorporating the necessary components for the potential of recruitment in the long-term, given that such views, if left unresolved and bolstered with negative emotions, can become taxing and problematic over time as previously discussed in chapter three. I stress here that this also fits into what we have discussed in our opening chapters concerning the 'likelihood that a child will suffer significant harm'; in these instances, it is left at the discretion and judgement of the worker to discern, and take action which should be proportionate to the seriousness of the risk perceived. On this point, it is also plausible to suggest that those involved in frontline delivery are constantly conducting 'observational risk assessment' (I believe that many can relate to this) and that any recordings from these observation must be shared to all

---

110 Partnerships in social care – a handbook for developing effective services, page 92.

those involved in a case given that such invisibilities can only become clearer through self-disclosure to others. Not surprisingly then, this brings us back to the common problem surrounding effective communication and information sharing between agencies that, at the best of times, have shown fundamental flaws. I would feel disappointed if their efforts, or the efforts of any individuals for that matter, were shattered through third-party negligence by connected services, and in this sense, we must conform to the line of reasoning presented by research that suggests multiple factors are at play.

Some researchers have observed some of these hindrances arising from aspects such as, *'delays with one sort or another, feedback on communication and problems relating to the professionals' roles, status and responsibilities'[111]*. In fact, as a means to overcome these problems, the need for professionals to engage in constant dialogue for the purpose of ascertaining information is of vital importance to towards strengthening this process. This point is serious and has been demonstrated with terrorist attacks that have succeeded on these grounds, because of some delay or failure of security services to act promptly having received viable and credible communication or intelligence in advance. This was exemplified with those involved in the July 7th attacks, where it was argued, this attack could have been prevented. For the reasons set forth, governing bodies, that have the sole responsibility for regulation and compliances (such as Ofsted) must deeply take these points on board. Organisations can no longer act on 'impulse' nor can they 'disregard' their role in this process especially in reference to inter-agency working and from safeguarding from extremism, in so far that professor Munro has stressed, in terms of service and state dependency, that, *'all children and young people are vulnerable to some extent by virtue of their age, immaturity and dependence on others particularly adults.'* She continues, *'the state's responsibility to protect children and young people means the government must continue to provide clear legal and regulatory framework and set out what vulnerable children and young people and families should expect from their collective efforts of local agencies'[112]*. In this consumption, it is only fair to say we have to consider other child-focused settings where children and young people are an integral part of the service provided and where openings might exist and where extremists may seek to exploit.

It is in the children's residential sector where we are reminded of the multidimensional challenges and problems associated with children and

---

111 Munro Review 2011.

112 Munro Review 2011.

young people in care, especially those looked after by Local Authorities and the private sector. Some of these concerns have been classified as anti-social and offending behaviour, absconding and, one of the most recent in media concerns, of child sexual exploitation (CSE). In addition to these, for those children and young people diagnosed with varying medical conditions (ADHD, autism) living within these establishments does not make matters any easier. What has been unforeseen by many employed or responsible for residential sectors, however, and which many may not be aware of, given the concerns of extremism recruitment, requires serious consideration. On this point, one registered manager of an established and leading UK child care provider, speaking on this subject, has repeatedly voiced, *'we must explore and take these issues and threats of extremism within residential settings more seriously, the risk to children and young people due to extremism has not been thoroughly explored'.* This requires a whole new dominance and is only the 'tip of the iceberg' for residential sectors.

Of course, it is here that Ofsted, the governing body responsible for the regulation of children's homes, must conduct their covert affairs in regards to inspection even more meticulously, given that the problems of extremism have the potential of existing and breeding in such 'fertile grounds'. Unfortunately, many Ofsted inspectors, compliance officers and others have at the best of times, lacked the expertise in recognising signs or patterns of extremism and furthermore many are without understanding of the tactics that could be deployed by extremists to infiltrate residential sectors, let alone the methods used by extremists to recruit children. This is even more disturbing, especially within our current climate, given the problems with ISIS grooming young people from within the UK. In terms of the regulation of these sectors, the National Minimum Standards and Children Homes Regulations 2001 were the bedrock legislation that informed many of the necessary steps to safeguard those within residential settings. The Care Standards Act 2000 is responsible as the primary source for ensuring that the regulation of services and provisions are maintained. For example, the National Minimum Standards (NMS) which derived from the CSA 2000 s(25) provided a clear set of measures, protocols and standards informing all providers delivering residential care to adhere to these in practice. I must inform the readers that current reviews are in the process of changing some of these procedures and processes and are set to be implemented in 2015. In short, the principle aims of standards are to promote;

'The child's welfare, safety needs should be at the centre of the care'.

The Secretary of State issues the NMS under s23 of CSA 2000 and they are regulated by Ofsted. The NMS standards are underpinned by the children's homes regulations 2001 and are therefore, statutory. It is intended that the standards will be used by providers and assessed by Ofsted to focus on seeing positive welfare, health, education outcomes for children, and reducing risks to their welfare and safety as an, *essential part of the overall responsibilities to safeguard and promote the welfare of each individual child*[113]. For example, Standard 4 of the NMS refers to provisions to *safeguarding children*. Given these safeguarding requirements in this sector, we must consider the wider implications that revolve around these vulnerabilities that are thriving in these settings, given our discussion in chapter four with respect to s11 of the Children Act 2004. One example referred to in section 11 to do with the 'absconding of children and young people' is certainly suggestive that extremists have some potential ground to gain in this sense. In these vulnerabilities, it is here that extremists, if they have reason to believe that in this landscape they can gain recruits, will pursue this venture to its materialisation. This then brings us back to the theoretical model discussed in chapter three in relation to 'breeding grounds' and 'cognitive openings'. In expounding on this point and taking into account the current concerns surrounding the Trojan horse plot, a spokesman for the Department for Education said, *'Ofsted inspectors would not go out specifically to look for extremism'* but added, *'Ofsted is working to ensure all inspectors have the necessary knowledge and expertise to determine whether extremist beliefs are being promoted in a school and then to take appropriate action'*[114]. A 'sharper focus therefore is required. In particular reference to residential sectors. Some examples of good practice spring to mind.

For those working within children residential sectors, the use of Schedule 5 referred in the regulations as 'events and notification' provides a valuable source of information sharing and communication. The aesthetic appeal of these schedules enables managers to inform Ofsted of any 'serious incidents or concerns' pertaining to a child or young person as they arise within these highly charged and dynamic settings. The registered manager of these establishments will then take the appropriate steps of notifying Ofsted regarding any serious concerns; these, according to a schedule of criteria, include absconding, serious accident or death. These existing measures further strengthen information sharing between agencies and are a viable tool, and in my view, will

---

113 www.ofsted.gov.uk
114 www.ofsted.gov.uk

have wider significance for the purpose of notification of extremism-related activity. Correspondingly, the use of schedule 6, '*Matters to be monitored by the registered person*' also has some operational relevance, which requires further exploration by Ofsted. The use of these and other systems can help manage the process of sharing of informing within residential sectors more effectively and can be further strengthened by a range of internal tools, for example, '*monitoring risk management*' and by '*incorporating relevant information into care or placement plans*'. These have positive connotations for inter-agency working, by informing others during or prior to any meeting pertaining to the child or young person status or being placed into care.

A WIDER ORIENTATION ON EXTREMISM AND INTER-AGENCY WORKING

The orientation of inter-agency working due to violent extremism and terrorism has gone to a wider field outside of local institutions. In this resurgence, Prevent professionals prepared themselves for wider engagements at local meetings within the community. One particular meeting, that has often been referred to as 'tension monitoring' opened the room for greater exposure. This formation has been largely influenced by the Crime and Disorder Act 1998. Its central theme and overall purpose was to reduce crime and was set to achieve this objective through 'joint tasking and building on experience that combines good practice from different partners into a coherent approach' in accordance with the Crime and Disorder Act 1998, especially from partners that could provide community-based solutions. This attracted a range of organisations and professionals.

Amongst those that have attended these meetings have included; local housing officers, local community wardens, community safety officers, youth offending teams, youth service and the police. It was because of this process and the aforementioned legislation, which enabled Prevent professionals to integrate themselves.

These meetings certainly provided the platform and impetus needed to exchange information. For example, if any concerns of a local groups' presence that threatened the harmonisation of communities because of extremism or use of violence, provided the ideal opportunity for external referrals to be actioned by Prevent professionals. Examples have been seen with the problems of 'far-right groups' that have certainly given rise to local conflicts. Some of the longstanding difficulties, in this sense, have been most prevalent between the Muslim community, the BNP and the EDL. These have been ripe in boroughs such as Sandwell, Dudley and Walsall. Other measures have been visible with

Prevent officers based in key locations.

Institutionally, referrals stemming from a diverse range of services situated under one roof, to Prevent workers, were also increased due to these and other factors. For example, organisations like youth offending teams have benefited from Prevent professionals located on the premises. Diachronically, additional services that were privileged and selected to come on board, were also given preferential treatment. Because of the youth offending services' wide remit, the range of professional services delivering interventions have included teams such as FIP (Family Intervention Project) DECCA (Drugs Education Counselling Alcohol) and TYS (Targeted Youth Support). In sharing some commonalities, the overall aims and objectives of some of these services were tasked to provide assessment and interventions particularly for the purpose of engaging children, young people and families at risk of some disadvantage. These covered a wide and comprehensive range of measures that sought to address issues such as anti-social and offending behaviour, parenting, education and unemployment, substance misuse and alcohol addiction. Crucially, a part of Prevent's role here, would incorporate informing those professionals and services to be cognizant of the troubling signs of extreme views or extremism activity, which may arise during their initial assessment or from their caseloads. Some were alienated by this and required reassuring. To relieve any anxieties and to restore confidence, Prevent workers provided the necessary support to ensure these apprehensions were dissipated. This was also necessary to ease any criticisms conceived regarding the purpose of Prevent in these establishments and to provide a balanced perspective.

The content from these and other referrals would form the basis to providing accurate and valuable information to funders, one being the Youth Justice Board. This information would help to determine and establish a range of statistical factors that would assist towards researching and analysing patterns and trends. This would include the following; ethnicity of young person, age, religion, gender, intervention used and referral source. The submission of information would feed into a central database. It is here, I postulate, that this information might have appeal to security services such as MI5 and presumably, MI6. It is precisely because of these practicalities and processes that have enabled Prevent to continue to build credibility through 'evidence based programmes' instead of just the political banter or under the false pretences of governmental promises that have given a wrong image of thriving success. It is here that government's recommendations, publication and policies would be challenged and evaluated against the formalities of practice. This again remind us that governments that 'prioritise performance demands' by under-mining matters where children and young people are susceptible to violent extremism, or terrorism, cannot be logically justified or accepted, as already discussed. Correspondingly, inter-agency practice has also been adopted in countries that have synchronised on similar programmes around extremism, as well as being the targets of terrorist attacks. On a final note, the efforts from all services must provide continuity at all times, as on the reverse, efforts of extremists who unequivocally remain undeterred by sharing what they have with like-minded individuals have both mobilised their forces and driven attainment forward to achieve this mandate, especially on a global scale. This cannot be managed or countered by systems and processes that have failed at the 'basic level of intervention'. A changed mindset is therefore required to move away from conventional norms towards preferred responses, templates and assessment. This is also a task and a key opportunity for the practitioner and professional to utilise a wide range of resources, skills and knowledge to their advantage; this will also sharpen their practice in the process.

INTERNATIONAL PERSPECTIVES

Collective security – a shared responsibility is the Norwegian Government's action plan to prevent radicalisation and violent extremism. The Norwegian Ministry of Justice and the police published the action plan in 2010. In conjunction with this, SaLTo is a collaborative model between the City of Oslo and Oslo Police District regarding the prevention of crime among children and young persons aged 12–22 years. The model was established in 2004 in some parts of the city and was implemented throughout Oslo as a whole in 2006. The preventative work regarding violent extremism is integrated within this model and is referred to in the central SaLTo action programme 2014–2017. Australia's approach has been apparent through education inter-vention, and has been ripe with the *'Beyond Bali Education Resource'* - funded by the Australian Government's Building Community Resilience Grants of the Federal Attorney General's Department - that applies a conceptual frame-work grounded in moral disengagement theory. Beyond Bali is a five module programme for schools that is specifically designed to build social cogni-tive resilience to violent extremism by engaging self-sanctions and preparing students to challenge the influence of violent extremism that can lead to moral disengagement. The theory of moral disengagement has been applied to the study of radicalisation to violent extremism to explain how individuals can cognitively reconstruct the moral value of violence and carry out inhumane acts. The mechanisms of moral disengagement through which individuals justify violence, dehumanise victims, disregard the harmful consequences of violence and absolve themselves of blame have been used in the construction of violent extremist narratives. However, they have not been applied to the development of intervention strategies that aim to counter the radicalising influences of violent extremist narratives

In America, the President, Federal Bureau of Investigation (FBI), Department of Homeland Security (DHS), and the National Counterterrorism Center (NCTC) are the most relevant elements of the U.S. government to the threat of American Islamic extremism and each has taken steps to address and counter the issue. Since 9/11 the government has worked to improve information sharing within the government, and between federal, state, local, and tribal law enforcement, as well as with the public. The 'If You See Something, Say Something' campaign, instituted by DHS and local law enforcement, was created to raise public awareness of the potential dangers. In August 2011, the Office of the President released a strategy to counter violent extremism called *Empowering Local Partners to Prevent Violent Extremism in the United States*. The strategy takes a three-pronged approach of community engagement, better training, and counter-narratives. In brief, this strategy states, *'We must actively and aggressively counter the range of ideologies violent extremists employ to radicalise and recruit individuals by challenging justifications for violence and by actively promoting the unifying and inclusive visions of our American ideals,'* challenging extremist propaganda through words and deeds. The goal is to *'prevent violent extremists and their supporters from inspiring, radicalising, financing, or recruiting individuals or groups in the United States to commit acts of violence'.* Other collaboration between countries that sought to promote partnership working and develop relationships has been key to establishing networks and counter extremism and terrorism. International crime fighting agencies have bought into such an approach.

Interpol chief advisors, in stressing the urgency of compliance within international relations, have stressed that, *'interpol can empower your front-line officers with access to the global tools and services they need to identify people in possession of the false identity documents that terrorists value so highly. We can help front-line officers make links between terrorism and other criminal activity. And we can expand the sharing of information on persons of interest among police in our 188 member countries'.* In the strengthening of international relations and with a focus on children and young people, many projects that are strongly supported by the US and EU Member States have a youth-focus and youth-led CSOs that provide a series of inter-related life skills from education and training to career advice and leadership of youth-led community projects. These efforts, which are targeted on young people aged between 15 and 25 years focus on education and training, leadership development, vocational training, peaceful conflict resolution, critical thinking and problem-solving, networking and positive civic contributions. Embedded in this are measures to deal with extremist narratives, recruitment, reverse marginalisation and dissatisfaction among young people.

Other countries where issues of terrorism are flourishing have followed suit. Most recruits to extremism in Pakistan are young individuals, where they are recruited to the Taliban but also to other extremist groups. Pakistani youth organisations are very active, especially those operating in urban areas. Their activities include campaigns to create awareness among the general public, public debates and efforts to promote sound education, including vocational education. Young individuals in Pakistan are at risk of radicalisation and recruitment to extremism and many young people are restless and disillusioned by their country's leadership, disheartened by the economic outlook and desperate for a radical change.

Conclusion

'In the UK, it will be communities that defeat terrorism and it remains our greatest challenge to support the development of communities that are wholly hostile to violent extremism and to identify, support and protect those who are vulnerable to extremism'

Miss Cressida Dick,
as Police Commissioner Metropolitan Police

By now the reader will have formed some opinions and raised critical questions or even absorbed what they have read as serious points for further consideration. Whatever the case, the evidence and facts from the various cited sources, publications and reviews have stated quite conclusively, extremism has now claimed new recruits, lives and territory, and by those who have targeted children and young people has posed a threat to all services, as currently seen with the actions of ISIS. In terms of these threats, many are unconvinced that this problem will go away by any stretch of the imagination, and which is where I stress that terrorism *'has a credible and growing presence in the United Kingdom, and will continue to have a certain future given that there will always be extremists, some that are bound to exercise their evil in the face of societies that promote democracy and liberty*. In continuing to expound on this point, the use of violence to propagate any message, be it political, religious or ideological, with a view to influence changes must be considered dangerous given what we have already established in this study and for those extremist which have opted for the use of violence have voluntarily become the agents of 'evil' and have clearly demonstrated their evils through the recruitment and radicalisation of those living within the UK to participate within acts of violence and terrorism against the state and towards anyone who are a threat to their way of life. For those who have used the name of the true God to become judge or jury by executing horrific acts of terrorism are also deluded by reason of their own convictions. These and other question then become available for the many social and child-care professionals who are aware of what needs to be done but the million dollar question being, what works to safeguard children and young people from extremism? There are also implications and challenges in regards to structures, process and policies that, quite arguably, are currently unexplored and not yet in existence. This needs a sharper focus. This has been an ongoing issue for most educational and child-focused establishments.

Almost a decade on from the 2005 terrorist attacks, the need to enforce counter-terrorism measures for prevention purposes, both for the short and long-term, was just the start to this innovative process. Since then, the Prevent strategy has provided some guidance, launching itself into an 'ocean of diverse and uncharted territory' with much land still to conqueror. In spite of how Prevent has been portrayed, it has gradually begun to gain the respect it deserved as a counter-terrorism approach and more pointedly as a safeguarding deterrent, which has already been discussed in chapters four and five. To date, it is also clear that Prevent has continued to make strides within a variety of disciplines. In terms of its longevity, it is the future that will dictate. It has also allowed the contribution of services and organisations to provide some expertise on counter-terrorism agendas that were initially lacking, importantly by keeping children and young people safe from the harm of extremism, as many services continue to refer cases under the auspices to the channel project under the banner of Prevent. On the other hand, lessons have been learnt in rushing polices and legislation that have at times proved counter-productive for communities, professionals and organisations. The catalogues of reviews contained with the research are a testament that a more structured, systematic and flexible approach is warranted, firstly, in safeguarding and secondly, preventing extremism. Crucially, this has also yielded insight to explore the wider dimension of abuse as a category of harm, which is inextricably linked to extremism and terrorism, as discussed already. This is still very much in its infancy stage. It goes without saying, the microcosm of extremists have exploited the younger generation by glamorising violence and further propagating that it is fashionable to hold extreme views, even if they are in conflict with the values or principles of British or western societies. My appraisal of the current situation is divided, for the reasons set forth in this research and is constantly forming. There must also be a platform given within theological and religious arenas that will enable those to address head on the issues of extremism and terrorism, be they Churches, Temples or synagogues. The expertise of those from Channel alone, are unable to meet these demands. There are also wider legal implication introduced by terrorism laws that are in the pipeline which have only be touched upon within this study and where there is a responsibility on professionals to respond will create further challenges and reforms. Some of these have been outlined in chapter four and five, but require research within itself to inform those at frontline.

In terms of prevention, it must be noted, not to mislead the readers, that the range of interventions discussed, as a means to disengage or deradicalise children and young people from extremism, are as much contested in themselves, with many that have strangely evaporated or disappeared. On the other hand, we can agree that, if it assists or fulfils the task at hand, then it has contributed towards tackling the wider problem, and thus minimised the risks to children and young people by prohibiting them to engage in violent acts or acts of terrorism, and therefore met safeguarding obligations in respect to protection from harm. On this point, Prevent has depended on the expertise of services to develop interventions to prevent children and young people engaging in violent extremism; and therefore at this time, in terms of counterterrorism measures, governments will continue with the 'gospel according to Prevent'. I am still dubious if this will be done purely through this medium, and in this sense, there is much work that needs to be done. A radical overhaul of management teams and structures are also required to secure into post those that have the relevant expertise to steer this in the right and preferred direction.

The task for professionals and organisations working to safeguard children and young people from extremism is to develop relevant frameworks within which they can develop effective systems as discussed in the previous chapter. Tailored assessments are therefore critical to this process and must also be considered outside of conventional formats such CAF and need to be bespoke according to the needs of the service and not according to government recommendation. A point already discussed is that many professionals are confined to making assessment due to dictation, which may not be effective on matters of extremism or terrorism, by virtue of the fact that not all problems affecting children are confined to some sociological or environmental factors as discussed from chapter one. This is clear with those that are driven by terrorism, which is political and religiously inspired.

Children and young people may hold extreme views that are similar to ideological ones upheld by terrorists that perpetuate negative meanings and that are similar in theory, functioning and purpose. These cannot be left ignored. Those engaged with children and young people must keep those individuals identified who harbour extreme views that are of a violent nature or and that might lead to violence, at close proximity and prevent them from contaminating others. They must be challenged on the content of their views, regardless of their origins or conceptions, and any use of violence or threat of the use of violence must be taken seriously. We must also be aware of the many strands to how the grooming and recruitment process can occur. Having discussed these in detail during chapter three, professionals should be aware of any significant triggers or behaviours that fall within these categories and immediately draw their attention to abnormal patterns. It is fair to say that only the worker will know the child and young person and at best, will be the surveillance to record or observe any sudden changes to their personality. Irrespective of the service, be it social service, education, youth work, youth justice, residential, CAMHS (Child and Adolescent Mental Health Services) or within psychology divisions the difficulty that we all have or that may arise is to adequately resource ourselves to respond. There are further implications for those employed in other sectors such as in British transport and aviation let alone in the public domain such as in shopping centres, retail and sport environments, tourism or at cinemas where numerous children and young people pass through There will always be opportunities for extremists to gain access to children and young people, and what we anticipate is whose child next? I also propose that young people are posing a threat to national security, which we have conclusively established in chapter two. This requires further research by experts and those with an appetite for counter-terrorism work, must possess the necessary knowledge, understanding, skills and expertise to adopt and adapt to this growing agenda and the demanding criteria to accomplish this task, which has proven a challenge even for security services such as MI5. It will only be a matter of time before, God forbid, the UK will wake up to hear of the first young British suicide bomber who has killed him or herself on British soil. This, is then, only the beginning of what is awaiting us in the years to come.

Select Bibliography

Akhtar, S. (1999) 'The Psychodynamic Dimension of Terrorism', *Psychiatric Annals,* vol. 29, no. 6, pp. 350 – 355.

Allen, Chris 'Islamphobia' (2010) 'University of Birmingham, UK. Ashgate Publishers, Surrey, UK.

Anonymous. "The Psychology of Terrorism." In *Security Digest*, 18. Washington: Wilson Center Reports, 1987.

AIVD (2002) *Recruitment for the jihad in the Netherlands*, The Hague: AIVD.

AIVD (20041) 'Background of Jihad Recruits in the Netherlands', General Intelligence and Security Service of the Netherlands (AIVD).

Benedek, E.P. *The Psychiatric Aspects of Terrorism*. Washington: American Psychiatric Association, 1980.

Bjorgo, T. (ed.) (2005) *Root Causes of Terrorism: Myths, Reality and Way Forward*, London: Routledge.

Bjorgo, Tore*, 'Terror from the Extreme Right'.* August 1995.

Cooper, H.H.A. "What Is a Terrorist? A Psychological Perspective," *Legal Medical Quarterly*, 1, 1977, 16-32.

Crenshaw, Martha. "The Causes of Terrorism," *Comparative Politics*, 13, July 1981, 379-99.

Crenshaw, Martha. "Current Research on Terrorism: The Academic Perspective," *Studies in Conflict and Terrorism*, 15, 1992, 1-11.

Crenshaw, Martha. "An Organization Approach to the Analysis of Political Terrorism," *Orbis,* 29, 1985, 465-89.

Crenshaw, Martha. "The Psychology of Political Terrorism." Pages 379-413 in Margaret Hermann, ed., *Handbook of Political Psychology*. San Francisco: Jossey-Bass, 1985.

Daly, L.N. "Terrorism: What Can the Psychiatrist Do?" *Journal of Forensic Sciences*, 26, 1981, 116-22.

Ellemers, N., R. Spears & B. Doosje (2002) 'Self and Social Identity', *Annual Review of Psychology, vol.* 53, pp. 161-186.

Elliot, John D., and Leslie K. Gibson, eds. *Contemporary Terrorism: Selected Readings.* Gaithersburg, Maryland: International Association of Chiefs of Police, 1978.

Elliott, Paul. *Brotherhoods of Fear: A History of Violent Organizations.* London: Blandford, 1998.

Fields, Rona M. "Child Terror Victims and Adult Terrorists," *Journal of Psychohistory*, 7, No. 1, Summer 1979, 71-76.

Fergus Smith & Professor Tina Lyon, 'The Children Act 1989' in the context of The Human Rights Act 1998 CAE (Children Act Enterprise), 2006, 5th Edition.

Franz, B. (2007) 'Europe's Muslim youth: An inquiry into the politics of discrimination, relative deprivation, and identity formation', *Mediterranean Quarterly,* vol. 18, no. 1, pp. 89-112.

Fresco, A., D. McGrory. & A. Norfolk (2006) 'Video of London Suicide Bomber Released', *Times Online*, 6 July.

General Intelligence and Security Service (AIVD), *Recruitment for the Jihad in The Netherlands: From Incidentto Trend*, Den Haag: AIVD, December 2002, 34.

Hacker, Frederick J. *Crusaders, Criminals, Crazies: Terror and Terrorism in Our Time.* New York: W.W. Norton, 1996.

Hacker, Frederick J. "Dialectical Interrelationships of Personal and Political Factors in Terrorism." Pages 19-32 in Lawrence Zelic Freedman and Yonah Alexander, eds., *Perspectives on Terrorism*, Wilmington, Delaware: Scholarly Resources, 1983.

Hassan Mahamdallie, 'Defending Multi-culturalism' a guide of the movement, Bookmarks publication, 2011.

Hudson, R.A. (1999) Sociology and Psychology of Terrorism: Who Becomes a Terrorist and Why? Guilford, C.T.: The Lyons Press.

Jenkins, Brian M. *High Technology Terrorism and Surrogate Warfare: The Impact of New Technology on Low-Level Violence.* Santa Monica, California: Rand, 1975.

Jenkins, Brian M. "International Terrorism: A New Mode of Conflict." In David Carlton and Carolo Schaerf, eds., *International Terrorism and World Security*. London: Croom Helm, 1975.

Jenkins, Brian M. "Terrorists at the Threshold." In E. Nobles Lowe and Harry D. Shargel, eds., *Legal and Other Aspects of Terrorism*. New York: 1979.

Jenkins, Brian M., ed. *Terrorism and Beyond: An International Conference on Terrorism and Low-Level Conflict*. Santa Monica, California: Rand, 1982.

King's College London. "The Internet." in *Recruitment and Mobilisation for the Islamist Militant Movement in Europe*. (University of London, December 2007), 89.

Kirby, A. (2007) 'The London Bombers as 'Self-Starters'. A Case Study in Indegenous Radicalisations and the Emergence of Autonomous Cliques', *Studies in Conflict & Terrorism,* vol. 30, no. 5, pp. 415-428.

Lake, D.A. (2002) 'Rational Extremism: Understanding Terrorism in the Twenty First Century', *International Organisation*, vol. 56, no. 1, pp. 15-29.

Maurice Ifran Coles, 'Every Muslim Child Matters' practical guidance for schools and childrens services, Trentham Books Limited, 2008.

Ministry of Foreign Affairs of Denmark (2007) *'Countering radicalisation through development assistance – A Country Assessment Tool'*, Copenhagen: Ministry of Foreign Affairs of Denmark.

Neil Moonie, Richard Chaloner, Kip Chan Pensley, Beryl Stretch, David Webb, 'Advanced Health and Social Care', Heinemann AVCE, 2000.

Paul A Singh, *Asian Adolesent in the west'* (1999) (BPS) British Psychological society, UK.

Post, Jerrold. "Current Understanding of Terrorist Motivation and Psychology: Implications for a Differentiated Antiterrorist Policy," *Terrorism*, 13, No. 1, 1990, 65-71.

Post, J.M. (1987) '"It's us against them": The group dynamics of political terrorism', *Terrorism,* vol. 10, pp. 23-35.

P.W. Singer, "The New Children of Terror," *The Making of a Terrorist: Recruitment, Training and Root Causes*, vol. 1, ed. James J.F. Frost, (Praeger, November 2005), 105-119.

Richard Ward and Olwen M Davies, 'The Criminal Justice Act 2003' A Practitioners Guide, New Law Series, Jordans Publishing, 2004.

Roy, O. (2004) *Globalised Islam: The search for a new Ummah,* New York: Columbia University Press.

Schmid, Alex P., and Albert J. Jongman. *Political Terrorism: A New Guide to Actors, Authors, Concepts, Data Bases, Theories, and Literature*. New Brunswick, New Jersey: Transaction Books, 1988.

Silber, M. D. & A. Bhatt. (2007) 'Radicalisation in the West: The Homegrown Threat', The New York City Police Department.

Stanley J. Grenz & Roger E.OSlson, 'Who Needs Theology' An invitation to the study of God, Inter Varist Press, 1996.

Stern, J. (2003) *Terror in the name of God: Why religious militants kill,* New York: Ecco.

Steve Hewitt, 'The British War on Terror' Terrorism and Counter-terrorism on the Home front since 9/11, Continuum, 2008, pg 119-122.

Strentz, Thomas. "A Terrorist Psychosocial Profile: Past and Present," *Law Enforcement Bulletin*, 57, No. 4, 1988, 11-18.

Taarnby, M. (2005) *Recruitment of Islamist Terrorists in Europe: Trends and Perspectives*, Aarhus: Centre for Cultural Research, University of Aarhus.

Dr. Gabriel Weimann, "The Internet as a Terrorist Tool to Recruit Youth" (presentation given at the Youth Recruitment & Radicalization Roundtable, Arlington, Virginia, March 19, 2009).

Wintrobe, R., 2006. Rational Extremism: The Political Economy of Radicalism. Cambridge : Cambridge University Press.

WEBSITE

MI5, www.**mi5**.gov.uk

MI6, www.sis.gov.uk

Cabinet Office, www.cabinetoffice.gov.uk

CIA, www.cia.gov

Interpol, http://www.interpol.int

FBI, http://www.fbi.gov

CPS, www.**cps**.gov.uk

Home Office, www.gov.uk/government/organisations/home-office

Ofsted, www.gov.uk/government/organisations/**ofsted**

Website reports

Tackling Extremism in the UK: Report from the Prime Minister's Task Force on Tackling Radicalisation and Extremism (December 2013) (London: HM Government): https://www.gov.uk/government/uploads/system/uploads/attachment_data/file/263181/ETF_FINAL.pdf

Prime Minister's Office (2013) 'Woolwich incidence – government response', 22nd May 2013: www.gov.uk/government/news/woolwich-incident-government-response

Home Office (2011) *Prevent* (London: Home Office): https://www.gov.uk/government/uploads/system/uploads/attachment_data/file/97976/prevent-strategy-review.pdf

Cameron, David (2011) *PM's Speech at Munich Conference*, 5-2-11: http://www.number10.gov.uk/news/pms-speech-at-munich-security-conference/

Ewan King (2011) 'Just out – the new, improved Prevent strategy', OPM blog 8th June 2011: www.opm.co.uk/just-out-the-new-improved-prevent-strategy/

Former Secretary of State at the DCLG, John Denham, recently reflected on new Labour's Prevent strategy suggesting: 'With no clear national guidance on forging allies against terrorism, mistakes were inevitable [...] Despite this, Prevent did good work in areas *where people worked through the challenges for themselves*' [emphasis added]. John Denham (2013) 'After Woolwich, we should not 'Prevent' certain views, but engage with them', *The Guardian*, 29th Mary 2013: http://www.theguardian.com/commentisfree/2013/may/29/after-woolwich-prevent-views-engage

The Thames Valley Police Report (2010) highlighted evidence of an explicit strategy of concealment of the counter-terrorism purposes of the cameras from the wider public. See also, Steve Jolly (2010) 'Birmingham's spy-cam scheme has had its cover blown', *The Guardian*, 23rd June 2010: http://www.theguardian.com/commentisfree/libertycentral/2010/jun/23/birmingham-spy-cam-scheme

Reviews

Birmingham Safeguarding Children's Board (2010). *Serious Case Review under Chapter VIII 'Working Together to Safeguard Children' in respect of the Death of a Child Case Number 14.* Birmingham Safeguarding Children's Board, Birmingham.

The Lord Lamming Review 2003 and 2009.

Every Child Matter – Consultation 2003.

The Munro Review of '*Child Protection Systems*', *Df*E, 2011.

Selected Journals, Articles, Newsletters and Report

'*A Decade lost, re-thinking radicalization and extremism*' Professor Aruni Kundai, Claystones.

Anonymous. "Terrorism: Psyche or Psychos?," *TVI Journal*, 3, 1982, 3-11.

Bell, J. Bowyer. "Psychology of Leaders of Terrorist Groups," *International Journal of Group Tensions*, 12, 1982, 84-104.

Baumeister, R.F. & Leary, M.R. (1995) 'The need to belong: Desire for interpersonal attachments as a fundamental human motivation', *PsychologicalBulletin*, vol. 117, no. 3, pp. 497-529.

Causal Factors of Radicalsation, Transnational Terrorism, Security and Law, 2008.

Community Care Magazine, January 2015.

Cyber-Terrorism: Legal principle and law in the United Kingdom, page 625, Professor Clive Walker (ethics of responding to terrorism).

DeMause, L. (2002) 'The childhood origins of terrorism', *Journal of Psychohistory*, vol. 29, no. 4, pp. 340 - 348.

Hamilton, L.C., and J.D. Hamilton. "Dynamics of Terrorism," *International Studies Quarterly*, 27, 1983, 39-54.

Prevent – Community Engagement Activity (A focus on Youth) Issues 1 August 2010.

The Australian News.

Thomas, Paul (2010) 'Failed and Friendless: The UK's 'Preventing Violent Extremism' Programme' in *British Journal of Politics and International Relations* (12, 3: 442-458).

HM and Government Publications

Building Partnerships, Staying Safe - The Healthcare Sector's contribution to HM Government's Prevent Strategy: for healthcare organisations. 2011.

Channel: protecting vulnerable people from being drawn into terrorism, a guide for local partnerships (October 2010).

Every Child Matters (Five Outcomes) United Nations Convention on the Rights of the Child (UNCRC) (UNICEF).

Every Child Matters 2003.

HM Prevent Agenda 2011.

Tackling Extremism in the UK: Report from the Prime Minister's Task Force on Tackling Radicalisation and Extremism (December 2013) (London: HM Government), p. 4.

The Department of Health (DoH) entitled *Assessment Framework Model implemented in 2000.*

HM 'what to do if you're worried a child is being abused' 2006.

HM 'Working Together to Safeguard Children' – 2006, 2010 and 2013.

HOME SELECT COMMITTEE

House of Commons Social services Select Committee 1984.

The House of Commons Education Committee fourth report and session 2012-13, *Children first: the child protection system in England.*

Claystone submission of evidence to Home Affairs Committee inquiry on Counter Terrorism – March 2014.

House of Commons Home Affairs Committee Roots of violent radicalisation Nineteenth Report of Session 2010–12

LEGISLATION

Care Standards Act 2000.

Crime and Disorder Act 1998.

Offence Against the Person Act 1861 s18.

The Children and Young Persons Act 1933.

The Children Act 1989, 2004.

The Children Home Regulation 2001.

The Terrorism Act 1974.

Terrorism Legislation, 2000, 2001, 2005 and 2006 and The Counter-Terrorism Security Act 2015

RELIGIOUS TEXTS

The Holy Bible - King James Version 1611.

The Quran.

NEWS SOURCES

The Times News Paper 2005.

The Daily Telegraph.

The Sunday Telegraph.

The Independent.

Russia Today.

Sangat TV.

BBC News (2005) 'London Bomber: Text in Full', 1 September.

BBC News (20061) 'Profile: Mohammad Siddique Khan', 11 May.

BBC News (20062) 'Video of July 7 Bomber Released', *BBC News Online*, 6 July, Panorama.

CONFERENCES, EVENTS AND TRAINING

Prevent 2009, ICC, Birmingham, West Midlands.

PVE –Preventing Violent Extremim, Youth Justice Board, 2009, level 1,2 and 3.

Course Handbook, The Recora Institute, 2010 (Translating research into policy and practice).

'*Prevent a Practitioner Perspective*' Conference, 2011, All Nations Consultancy, Tally Ho, Birmingham, West Midlands.

'Addressing The Many Forms of Violent Extremism' Conference, 2012, Birmingham, West Midlands.

'Prevent, Policy and Legislation', Seminar event, 2013 Joint University of Buckingham and All Nations Consultancy.

CONSULTATIONS

Prevent Consultation, Birmingham, December 2010.

Terrorism Legislation Review, Birmingham, September 2010.

Lightning Source UK Ltd.
Milton Keynes UK
UKOW06f1808140916

283002UK00025B/587/P